"There are two kinds of hunters and anglers: you've got the ones who stay home and complain about crowds or the weather or how everything's changed since they were a kid; and then you've got the ones who get out there and have a blast and make the action happen. Christi Elliott is the second kind, and I love following her adventures. *Always Game* demonstrates the power and happiness of an outdoor life."

—Steven Rinella, author and host of the MeatEater Podcast

"With her trademark honesty and humor, Maine native Christi Elliott welcomes readers into her life in the great outdoors, sharing her experiences on adventures like thru-hiking the Appalachian Trail, fishing for mahi-mahi on the U.S. Virgin Islands, hunting deer and trapping beavers in rural Maine, and, through it all, showing what it means to be a proud and successful woman hunter. *Always Game* is the next chapter in Maine's proud history of outdoorswomen and the next step in the legacy they are leaving for our daughters and granddaughters to follow."

—Janet Mills, Governor of Maine

"When I read outdoor memoirs, I always hope to find something new and interesting. I'm looking for turns of phrase that separate good writing from great writing, descriptive elements that lift the book out of the ordinary. Christi Elliott's debut, *Always Game*, is a piece of great writing. I'm both happy for the author and a touch envious at what she has accomplished here. Well done, Christi. This is a wonderful read."

—Jim Shockey, outfitter, author, and television producer

"I have known Christi long enough to know that she is the real deal outdoorswoman. She is up for any adventure in the outdoors and takes them on full speed. Let Christi take you on her adventures in this book."

—Hal Blood, Master Maine Guide, author, and co-founder of Big Woods Bucks

"A registered Maine guide, influencer, hunter, angler, trapper and civil engineer, Christi Elliott has already accomplished a great deal in her young life. In *Always Game*, she shares her story, starting with her thrifty upbringing in Machias, then as a high school basketball stand-out, world traveler, Appalachian Trail thru-hiker, and leader of outdoorswomen. Her relaxed, straightforward writing style makes this book a delightful and inspirational read."

—Will Lund, editor, *The Maine Sportsman*

ALWAYS GAME

A Maine Woman's Life of
Outdoor Adventure

Also from Islandport Press

Moon in Full
Marpheen Chann

The Ghosts of Walter Crockett
W. Edward Crockett

Dear Maine
Morgan Rielly and Reza Jalali

Take It Easy
John Duncan

Whatever It Takes
May Davidson

Ghost Buck
Dean Bennett

This Day in Maine
Joseph Owen

Downeast Genius
Earl Smith

ALWAYS GAME

A Maine Woman's Life of
Outdoor Adventure

Christi Elliott

Christi Elliott

ISLANDPORT PRESS

ISLANDPORT PRESS

Islandport Press
247 Portland Street, Building C.
Yarmouth, Maine 04096
www.islandportpress.com

First Edition: 2025
Printed in the United States of America.
All photographs, unless otherwise noted, courtesy of Christi Elliott.

ISBN: 978-1-952143-24-3
Library of Congress Control Number: 2021935314

KJ Grow | Publisher
Dean L. Lunt | Editor
Emily Lunt | Book Designer
Teresa Lagrange | Cover Designer

Cover Image by Melissa Goodwin

For Mom and Dad

TABLE OF CONTENTS

INTRODUCTION
CHANGING THE FACE OF HUNTING

Christi Elliott is one of the most accomplished outdoorswomen I have ever been fortunate enough to know. She hunts—big game, small game, ducks, pheasants, turkeys—pretty much anything with a season. Not only does she trap animals, but she utilizes those animals to make jewelry and hats and mittens. She fishes all year long. She forages—for mushrooms, fiddleheads, and berries. She once confided to me that she keeps a spreadsheet of the calendar year with all the seasons mapped out so she doesn't ever forget or miss a season. But all that is just a small piece of her story. Christi is much more than an accomplished outdoorswoman—she is a movement, a phenomenon, a powerhouse, an influencer, a mentor, and an amazing friend.

In 2018, Christi started the Maine Women Hunters Facebook page. I came across the page one evening while scrolling through Facebook and immediately joined. The pictures were so inviting, so welcoming. They featured women I wanted to be friends with, people I'd like to hunt with. The group was the opposite of so many other social media groups I have seen.

Fast forward a few weeks and I met her at a meeting. I told her, "Oh, I think I just joined your group."

"Ya you did!" she replied so excitedly you would have thought I was someone famous. We talked after the meeting, and she immediately offered to take me turkey hunting. I happily accepted.

We did not harvest any turkeys that cold, crystal-clear morning, but as we sat shivering, we got to see the most beautiful sunrise. We basked in the morning sun watching warblers migrate along the edges of the field. We bonded in a way that you can really only do with someone while hunting.

Since that day, Christi's Facebook group has grown to more than seven thousand followers, and unlike many other social media groups that focus on hunting, her group is supportive, positive, helpful, and engaged. Not only do members support each other on social media but Christi organizes outings—ice fishing, rabbit hunting, skeet shooting, striper fishing, canoe trips—and opens them up to everyone. She created a group logo and offers merchandise that makes it easy to recognize other members.

The number of women who hunt and fish in Maine is growing. Maine now boasts one of the highest license renewal rates among women in the country, with women buying licenses as frequently as men. I am convinced this growth is because of the community support that exists in Maine, largely due to Christi's group and the encouragement it provides to members new and old. Learning to hunt is not easy, but Maine Women Hunters gives women a place to connect, a place to see like-minded women hunting, a place to ask questions, and a place to learn.

Growing up in Downeast Maine, Christi was no stranger to the outdoors, but her family did not hunt, so she learned on her own. She is one of the most curious people I have ever known, often asking a million questions, which is part of her charm. She's game for everything, as she is always eager to learn and experience anything. She shows up on time, bringing her gear and extra supplies just in case someone needs something. Shy is not a word to describe Christi. About anything. Her social media posts get attention for a reason. She's funny, sometimes she's racy, she's always smart, quick-witted, and, of course, she's drop dead gorgeous. She's the real deal—genuine, kind, sincere, passionate, welcoming, inclusive, committed, and generous.

The stories in this book recount her beginnings as a kid growing up in Maine and many of her successful and unsuccessful adventures as an adult. Collectively, her stories tell the tale of a woman on a mission, a path not many people take. They are sometimes laugh-out-loud funny, sometimes heart-wrenching, and always entertaining. They are stories that we all can relate to whether you hunt or fish or hike or canoe. And if you don't participate in any of these activities, her stories will grab you and will pull you into the outdoors with her.

Christi has created an outdoor community for women, a place for anyone wanting to learn, a place especially for those who haven't had the opportunity before. Her willingness to share her passion and knowledge, her time and energy, and even her favorite hunting and fishing spots will leave a lasting impact on you and Maine. Christi has changed the face of hunting, and quite frankly, it's about time!

Judy Camuso
Commissioner
Maine Department of Inland Fisheries and Wildlife

Christi Elliott and Judy Camuso visiting a bear den site. Wildlife technicians visit the dens of collared sows across the state every winter to evaluate and collect health information. This data helps them to maintain a stable bear population.

I CAN'T WRITE THIS BOOK

I can't write a book.

It's hunting season and an eight-point whitetail buck that must top two hundred pounds is showing up on my game camera. He shows up mostly at night, but still . . . The only two things stopping me from sitting in my deer stand every day, all day, waiting for that buck are work and the need, occasionally, to sleep.

On days when I hunt, which is every day I possibly can, I wake at five and drive through the morning darkness to Windham where I climb eighteen feet up a pine tree to sit in my ladder stand. I am there in time to watch the sunrise over a nearby cornfield.

In the gathering light, I see hooded mergansers whistle past me and glide down to water-landings on a nearby pond, and I hear chickadees chirping from the branches surrounding me. I watch for movement in the cornfield, but any movement I see is usually just crows or maybe a turkey pecking around for leftover corn. Hunting requires so much waiting and watching.

Finally, when I can't wait for that buck any longer because I want to remain employed, I climb back down and drive fifteen minutes to Gorrill Palmer in South Portland, where I sit in a cubicle working as a civil engineer drafting land development plans. I change out of my hunting gear in the parking lot so nobody at work sees me in full camouflage.

Once I get to work, it is hard for me to sit at my desk and focus, especially on beautiful fall days when the weather is cool and the winds are light. I can't stop thinking about that eight-point buck. I am paranoid that if I don't go out hunting every day, I will miss my opportunity to take him. The workdays seem to pass so slowly, but I steal some extra daylight hours by using vacation time to leave work by two o'clock. That gives me time to change back into my camo and race back to the tree stand, where I again sit and wait, this time watching until darkness engulfs me. Sometimes, I intentionally focus and mentally try to make that big buck materialize at the edge of the field. I haven't succeeded—yet.

By the time dusk settles in, I am tired—these are long days. Regardless, I know I'll repeat the same routine tomorrow. I'll again be angry at the sound of my early morning alarm but excited and hopeful that *this* is the day my deer hunting luck will change.

In the darkness, I carefully descend the ladder and walk to my truck using the beam from my headlamp. I drive home, heat a frozen pepperoni pizza in the oven, and fall into bed, mustering barely enough energy to say *goodnight* to my husband Travis.

I can't write a book.

I am just too busy.

I recently found a buck head from a twelve-pointer that died. I still need to boil it and whiten it so I can give it to the landowner as a gift. And I trapped a gray fox last week that is still sitting in my freezer waiting for me to skin and flesh it.

I am sure once I get a buck—that big eight, I hope—I will have more time to write. Although, I do have doe tags, too. And soon it will be Thanksgiving so I'll head home to Machias, at least a three-hour drive from my place in Gray, to visit my parents. Mom will cook turkey, squash, potatoes, peas, and make pumpkin pie for dessert. She will complain about the deer that bed in her backyard, which is right in the middle of town, and tell me that they have eaten all three of her rhododendron bushes. I have a doe tag there, too. I wish I could just hunt in her backyard, but there are too many houses nearby. (Plus, that wouldn't be very sporty.)

In December, after deer season has ended, I will have more time to write. Although, by then I'll be working forty hours a week again—not including my thirty-minute daily commute each way. I'll also jump back into my one-hour workout routine at OrangeTheory, lifting weights and running intervals on the treadmill. I'll return to cooking real meals, hopefully using venison (maybe from that big eight-point buck!) like stir fry, chili, spaghetti, and shepherd's pie. I'll spend more time with Travis, who is also busy managing Sullivan Tire in Falmouth. I can't forget to order Christmas cards. After a day of working, exercising, commuting, showering, cooking, eating, and cleaning—it will be time for bed.

And I will not have time to write a book. I will be exhausted.

Maybe I'll write more after my birthday, which falls on Christmas Eve. We don't really celebrate my birthday as a birthday because it's already such a busy time of year. Of course, this year, I have some homeowner problems to take care of as well. The hot tub is running cold, so I need to call and make an appointment to fix it. We need to blow leaves in the yard and take out the dock before the lake freezes. And we need to winterize our boat so it's in good shape and ready to go when the ice melts come spring and the brookies, browns, and rainbows chase alewives just beneath the surface.

I'm dog-sitting Koko, my friend Meg's mixed hound, and farm-sitting for my friends with chickens this weekend. Maybe I can write there.

And it's not like I am not already writing— I've been writing a monthly column for *The Maine Sportsman* for years. When I was first asked to write a monthly column for the magazine, I was flattered but also concerned about the pressure. Not just pressure to meet deadlines, but I would be the only female columnist. Being in a minority also comes with added scrutiny. I take things personally so it's hard when I hear from readers that they didn't like my point of view on trapping, or they question whether I did something or if my husband did it for me. But I keep writing because I recognize the importance of normalizing women in the outdoors and being a role model to other women and girls.

As silly as it seems, one of my motivations to become a Registered Maine Guide was so I would garner more respect from strangers. I have had fishing laws mansplained to me, and once had an employee at Cabela's ask me if I was buying a game camera to "spy on my boyfriend." A Maine Guide is a licensed outdoor professional who can charge a fee to take clients hunting, fishing, or recreating. To become a Guide, you must pass an extensive exam consisting of a written test, map and compass, and an intimidating hour-long oral exam administered by game wardens or Master Maine Guides. I wanted to get my guide license so I could help other women learn to be confident in the outdoors.

After I got my hunting and fishing guide license, I started the Maine Women Hunters group on Facebook. I modeled it after the Maine Women Fly Fishers group, because I saw how helpful it was and thought it was even more important to have a community for women who hunted because there are fewer of us. I knew that if I was struggling learning how to hunt, other women were also struggling or, worse, just not getting involved. I mean, in hunting, you are handling firearms. You are dealing with the fact that you are taking a life. And there are a bajillion rules. My idea was to create a scrutiny-free place for women to ask questions and share stories.

I started the group by inviting my handful of female friends who hunted. In the beginning, there was not much action in the group, so I would post prompts asking for recipes, or photos of members' hunting dogs. Initially, it was just a fun place to share hunting photos and ask questions.

But it grew quickly and today the group has over seven thousand members that go on outings. I met all my close friends through the group. Sometimes men are upset that they're not allowed in the group and threaten facetiously, "I'm going to make a group for men only," and I reply that it's a free country, and to go ahead. It's important to keep the group a safe space for women. Women hunters have different questions than men, and men can sometimes be condescending about them. For example, women have questions that relate to hunting while pregnant, hunting while having periods, where to buy women's hunting clothes, what guns are best for petite women, etc. On other hunting sites, people can be rude and judgmental or hit on a woman who posts a photo. I think some guys don't remember when they learned how to hunt because they were eight years old. Encouragement is crucial. Maine Women Hunters encourages women to embrace their wild and dirty side and help empower them to bring an important new voice to the sport.

I'm not sure what the future of the group entails—offering scholarships, or becoming a non-profit perhaps, but for now I'm content organizing one trip per month, and empowering women to get outside.

Maybe I can write this book on Sundays.

You can't legally hunt on Sundays in Maine. It's a law that some keep trying to change, but it keeps getting voted down. However, Sundays are when I manage the Maine Women Hunters Facebook and Instagram pages, the Big Buck Contest, and logo store, and when I plan and manage events—the list goes on. When did I become this busy? When will I get a vacation?

I also need to make plans for the Maine Sportsman Show—book a hotel room, pay for my booth fee, figure out and order apparel to sell, make signs, enter the apparel items online, prepare for the

Members of the Maine Women Hunters group on a partridge hunt in Hodgdon.

seminars I will present, like "Intro to Beaver Trapping" or "Women in the Outdoors."

I don't have time to write a book.

My dad—Lyman Holmes, ever the realist—is skeptical anyway. *You're too young to write a book*, he tells me. Sometimes I believe him. He tells me not to stress so much about it. *Don't take on too much,* he says. My mom—Carlene Holmes, my cheerleader—has no doubts;

she encourages me to always say yes and to keep my options open. She says that after I finish this book, I'll just have to write a sequel in a few years. I'm not sure I believe either one of them.

It's not that I doubt myself or my ability to write a book, it's just that I've never written one before. I've taught myself how to fish, how to trap, how to hunt birds and deer and moose, but I've never set my sights on writing a book. It seems hard writing a memoir, hard digging up long-ago memories and remembering them clearly. How do other writers do that?

Yes, it's an honor that a publisher has asked me to write a book, to write my story. I have friends who have written books and self-published them, but that sounds like so much work.

Maybe writing down all my stories will give me solace when I read them later on, when I'm too old to climb up into my tree stand. Maybe my children will read this book as adults and will better understand the life their mother led; it may give them something they can hold on to. And maybe writing this book will help me understand how I got here, how I became so busy, and what drives me. Maybe it will help me understand how I've evolved, more and more, into the person and hunter I am today.

It is absolutely true that I don't have time to write this book. But I will. I have set my sights on it and am taking aim.

MY FIRST SOLO HUNT

With each step I took, gravel crunched loudly—too loudly—beneath my boots. I needed to move more quietly. I moved to the center of a long-retired logging road in Washington County where I could walk along a strip of grass growing between old tire tracks. For those who are looking for this road, a Bud Light can stuck on a bush marks its entrance off Route 9—The Airline, as locals call it. I wondered what this road looked like when loggers were using it. What did this area look like before any roads were built at all? I kept walking quietly, carefully, a borrowed Remington 870 pump-action 12-gauge slung over my shoulder, loaded with birdshot, a wide spread of pellets. Hoping to spot a ruffed grouse —King of the Game Birds (although the bird is better known as a partridge here in Maine), my eyes scanned roadside ditches and tree branches still covered with orange and red leaves.

Partridge eat gravel to help them digest food, so walking quietly along gravel roads is an effective method of hunting, or so I'd been told. This was my first solo hunt for partridge. I kept scanning the gravel swaths for any sign of life.

1

I jumped across a washed-out culvert. The lumber company that owns this old road would likely repair it in ten or so years when the planted spruce trees grow large enough to harvest. But until then, I will hunt here and not worry that a logging truck will rumble by and scatter the birds I'm searching for.

————————

At the time I was walking down the old logging road, I was twenty-five, living at home with my parents in Machias and working at the local engineering firm. I was fresh out of hunter's safety class. For the class, Amy, my childhood best friend, and I sat in a classroom for three days listening to old men tell rambling hunting stories. It seemed to me they liked telling stories more than they liked teaching. Regardless, we learned about hunting laws, hypothermia, how to load and unload shotguns, and the ins and outs of bolt-action and lever-action rifles. We learned about firearm safety, the need to positively identify game before firing, and survival tips if we become lost in the Maine woods.

We also learned about necessary conservation work and how it is funded. The government generates money by selling hunting licenses and places a special tax on such things as firearms and ammo. This money is used to create outdoor recreational access for everyone and wildlife research and habitat improvements—not just deer and turkeys, but butterflies and turtles, too.

There is also the Federal Duck Stamp program, for example. All waterfowl hunters must buy a twenty-five-dollar stamp annually, and nearly all of that money goes directly toward purchasing and protecting wetlands. To date, the Duck Stamp program has raised more than one billion dollars and conserved more than six million acres. Waterfowl aren't the only beneficiaries of increased wetlands; a slew of wildlife from frogs to muskrats to falcons to fish also depend on this habitat. The wetlands themselves also improve water quality and make it possible for people to enjoy bird watching.

———————

I chose to become a hunter even though no one in my immediate family hunted or fished—or even owned a gun. My great-grandfather was the last hunter in my family. My friend Amy's family didn't hunt either, not legally at least, but she was familiar with killing animals for food. Amy's mom, a four-foot, eleven-inch tall spitfire of a woman with a thick British accent, would grab her 22-caliber rifle and shoot any animal that wandered into her large vegetable garden. The family also raised chickens and geese for eggs and food. One weekend when I was still in middle school, I stayed with Amy. In the morning, we walked out to the family's chicken pen to collect eggs. I stayed outside the fence—I got a little nervous watching those hens—while Amy handed me the eggs. Suddenly, a large, white, honking goose bit Amy on her calf. She dashed out of the pen crying and we raced back to the house. After Amy's mom heard what happened, she grabbed a large kitchen cleaver and marched toward the pen, shouting, "I'll show that goose to bite my daughter!"

That night, we ate goose for dinner.

———————

When I was growing up in the 1990s and early 2000s, some people might say I was a bit of a goody two-shoes—I didn't get into much trouble, I was class valedictorian, I was the prom queen, and I was a basketball star at Machias Memorial High School. At the University of Maine at Orono, I was a straight-A student majoring in civil engineering as well as the homecoming queen.

During college and after I graduated in 2010, I explored the world for a bit.

I waited tables in the Virgin Islands, spent a summer in Acadia National Park, backpacked in Europe, and studied Spanish in Central America. I also worked as a ranch hand on a five-thousand-acre cattle ranch in Montana, went salmon fishing in remote parts of Alaska, and hiked the entire Appalachian Trail from Georgia to Maine. Every night for five months on the trail, I slept outside and lived off what little I carried in my pack.

It was all great fun. But these days, I spend most days sitting at my desk and working as an engineer.

And yet, here I was walking alone through the Maine woods, carrying a shotgun over my shoulder, and hoping to shoot a partridge. How did that happen?

For one thing, I like the feeling. When I am alone in the woods, I feel wild and alive. I love the heart-pounding excitement of the hunt. I appreciate the simplicity and quiet solitude (okay, boredom) of watching and waiting. I also crave independence.

Hunting also appeals to me for much more practical reasons—I want to source my own meat. When I was younger, my outdoor-enthusiast friends—grade school friends Isaiah and Austin, for example—made hunting look easy. They ventured out into the woods each fall, shot a deer, butchered it, and were then able to eat local, ethically sourced meat from their freezer all year. I liked the idea of harvesting wild game. I had eaten plenty of partridge harvested by my friends. They usually cut the breast meat into strips, fried it, and served the strips dipped in buffalo sauce. Partridge meat was tender and heavenly, better than chicken—the "veal of chicken," they liked to call it.

Anyway, I felt partridge hunting was a good place for me to start and this year I was determined to become a *real* hunter. Deer season was still a month away, and before it ended, I planned to fill my freezer with venison (I didn't). That was in the future, but at this particular moment, I was searching for partridge along this old logging road. It was the first step of many steps to come.

I kept walking and walking, and the sun rose higher and higher and kept getting in my eyes, somewhat blinding me. Suddenly, I heard a thunder of wings. The noise made me flinch. It sounded like a partridge and, in just a few flaps, the bird soared into a maple tree thirty yards ahead of me and disappeared.

I walked toward it, trying to keep my eyes on the spot where I had last seen the bird. Did it land in the tree or keep flying? After searching for what felt like an hour (but was probably only a couple of minutes), I gave up. I berated myself for being too slow, for missing my opportunity. But still, discouraged and scolding myself, I walked on.

I didn't like to lose.

Twenty yards down the road, a small, alert head periscoped in the center of a clearing.

Another bird.

It froze.

I froze.

I slowly lifted the 12-gauge shotgun to my shoulder. Then, just as I practiced in hunter's safety class, I clicked off the safety, aimed the front sight at the bird, fingered the trigger, and squeezed it.

Although new to hunting, I was no stranger to the woods. I grew up in Machias, a Washington County town of two thousand residents about thirty miles from the Canadian border. As the county seat, Machias is home to the county courthouse (where both my parents worked) and the county jail. Machias was also home to the only McDonald's and the only major grocery store, Shop 'n Save, within forty-five miles. We had no skate park or shopping mall. Our one tennis court included six-inch cracks from which sprouted grass high enough and thick enough to hide garter snakes, or at least that's what the older kids warned.

Entertainment options and organized activities were scarce; doing most anything required a long drive. Some of my classmates lived up to thirty minutes away. My swimming lessons and orthodontist were over an hour away in Ellsworth. The Bangor airport was a two-hour drive. All these years later, I still don't think twice about driving an hour to do something—to fish or hunt, for example. Long drives are just a way of life in rural Maine.

Whatever Machias lacked in organized activities, it made up for in undeveloped wild woods and waters. As kids, my older brother Martin and I often hiked thirty minutes or so into Munson's Pitch, part of the Machias River, where we repeatedly slid on our butts down the small rapids before hiking back home, soaking wet. On weekends, our family sometimes explored nearby Roque Bluffs State Park or drove to Acadia National Park, or headed to Cathance Lake to stay in a cabin built by my great-grandfather. The two-story cabin had no running water, but we spent every August living in it.

A train track ran through our neighbor's backyard. The train stopped running two years before I was born. Past the train tracks were acres of rolling fields, and a marsh fed by the tidal Machias River. We called it The Pastures, although I never knew it to be used by any livestock. As kids we played on the defunct tracks and went sledding on the small hills of The Pastures. Through my bedroom window, I listened to coyotes yip at night and enjoyed a peepers' chorus every spring.

It wasn't until I finished hiking the Appalachian Trail that I really started to consider hunting. I had grown disappointed by the conditions faced by livestock and the shadiness of America's factory farming practices. I felt guilty being a part of that system. It was just too easy to shirk responsibility for making things better when buying dyed red meat that barely resembled the animal it once was.

Hunting appealed to me because it forced me to face the serious impact of eating meat—to face the realities of taking a life for my own sustenance. Wild game is organic, free range, fresh, local, and entails minimal suffering. There isn't a more ethical way to eat meat.

So I set my sights on becoming a hunter. I am a very determined person by nature. I wasn't intimidated that hunting and fishing are male-dominated activities (so is engineering for that matter). And it didn't bother me that the entire outdoor industry was also dominated by men. After all, I also knew that the skewed balance was changing. In 2011, women accounted for just 10 percent of all licensed hunters in Maine. By 2022, that percentage had climbed to 15.1 percent.

In my case, my youth also helped me prepare to live in these male-dominated worlds. Growing up in a small town in rural Maine, you often bent gender norms out of necessity and thought nothing of it. Our high school, for example, was too small to have a girls' soccer team, so the girls played on the boys' team. When an adult once asked what I wanted to be when I grew up, I answered confidently, "The first female President."

Having an older brother meant I did everything he did, regardless of stereotypical gender expectations. I felt anything he could do, I could do, too, and no one told me I couldn't just because I was a girl. My brother and I were competitive. We turned everything into a competition. We raced razor scooters, we timed how long we could balance on an inflatable tube at the lake, and we strived to be the first one to learn to snap their fingers. He was older and smarter, but for the most part, I kept up.

———

I also leaned on the fact that when it comes to the outdoors, Maine has a lengthy history of accomplished outdoors women. In fact, one particular Maine woman—Cornelia "Fly Rod" Crosby,

Maine's first Registered Maine Guide in 1897—helped put our state's outdoor resources on the map. An avid fly fisherman, hunter, and outdoor writer, Crosby was a superb ambassador for Maine's outdoor heritage. She guided in the Rangeley area and is rumored to have shot Maine's last legally harvested caribou.

Carrie Stevens, who lived in the Rangeley area, was also an accomplished fly fisherman and astute fly tier. She invented the Gray Ghost streamer fly pattern in the early 1900s, and it remains one of the most popular trout and salmon flies today.

When I was in high school, I looked up to Linda Greenlaw of Isle au Haut. She was America's only female swordfishing captain and still fished for lobsters off the coast of Maine.

Judy Camuso became Maine's first female Commissioner of Inland Fisheries and Wildlife in 2019.

When I started to hunt and fish seriously, knowing about these women motivated me to carry on the traditions they'd help start. ·

Of course, I made mistakes. I once sat in a self-climbing tree stand in the predawn darkness, only to discover when the sun rose that it was barely twelve feet off the ground—so low it scared away whatever I was trying to hunt. I've battled seasickness all night and all day fishing for bluefin tuna in the Gulf of Maine. I once had to go number two so badly while sitting in a turkey blind that I did just that, surrounded by hen turkeys.

But I wouldn't trade any of it. These passions of mine allow me to enjoy the outdoors, to study and learn about wildlife, and to unplug and exist in the moment, which is a rare thing these days. Modern-day life often feels sterile, and full of comforts—warmth, cleanliness, access to food of all types. I realize hunting and fishing also causes suffering—to the species I target, and to myself. Hunting causes discomfort—you're often cold, bored, hungry, and discouraged. You have to move slowly, if at all, so you can blend in and not be seen first. You must have so much patience and optimism.

Experiencing hardship and overcoming adversity provides me with satisfaction. I love that hurts-so-good feeling after a long day in the woods and then dragging out a freshly harvested doe. Hunting teaches grit, discipline, humility, perseverance, and resourcefulness. I strive to take clean, ethical shots. And you get to see some pretty damn cool things while you're at it.

———————

So, back to the first solo hunt I took in 2013 along that deserted logging road. After I had spotted the partridge and squeezed the trigger, I found the bird lying on a soft bed of spruce needles. I walked to the bird, lifted it, and admired its downy feathers. I was surprised at how soft it was.

I had done it!

My first successful hunt.

My first step toward independence.

My first step toward becoming a real hunter.

Back home, I snapped a photo of the bird and texted it to my neighbor, Marco.

Got one! I texted.

I was so proud of myself.

Marco, an avid hunter, texted me back: *That looks a little dark . . . is there red near its eye?*

I inspected the bird's face. *Yeah! Why?*

Marco responded, *You better eat it quick, and they don't taste good! That's not a partridge, it's a spruce grouse and you're not allowed to shoot them!*

Maybe teaching myself to hunt was going to be more difficult than I thought.

1
GROWING UP DOWNEAST

I spent my entire childhood living in the same home, a two-story, three-bedroom, red house with white trim at 49 Center Street in the middle of Machias. My parents, now in their late seventies, still live there. Mom taught me to remember our address like this: Our home number, 49, was like the San Francisco 49ers football team, and the team's primary color was also red. That was the only time anyone ever talked about football in our household.

My dad's family settled in Machias from Scarborough in 1765, two years after the settlement was created by other people from Scarborough. I guess that makes us true locals.

Compared to my father's family, my mother's family were latecomers to America, not arriving until the late 1800s. My Polish ancestors settled in the coal mining area of Pennsylvania. My Irish ancestors settled in Lubec. My maternal grandparents met at Stewart Air Force base near Newburgh, New York, where my grandfather built and repaired airplanes and my grandmother did office work. They married at the end of World War II. My grandfather landed a job as a tool and die maker at IBM. The family moved to Lexington,

Kentucky with IBM (IBM stood for "I've been moved," as the Yankees joked). While living in Kentucky, they returned to Maine regularly to visit family, where my mom went lobstering, raked blueberries, and hiked with her Downeast cousins.

My mom, Carlene Marcinek, was the oldest of eight children. She became a high school foreign language teacher and traveled to Europe. In the sixties, Mom burned her bra, grew a garden, and coveted her well-worn copy of Rachel Carson's *Silent Spring*. It was on a trip to visit her family in Lubec that she met my father. Her Aunt Pat blocked the doorway, exclaiming to my mom and her cousin, "No supper until you take Carlene to meet Lyman Holmes."

Being hungry, the girls made a dooryard stop at Lyman's house and the two agreed to meet later at 5 Water Street. That night, the band played bluegrass and the moon was full. Dad swept my mother off her feet and the rest is history.

Strangely, I think, despite my mom's hippy past, she wouldn't let me cut or dye my hair while I was growing up. In middle school, my classmate Samantha got two blond highlights that framed her face. It was the phase of experimentation, but I couldn't participate. Instead, every morning Mom brushed and braided my hair into two neat braids like Wednesday Addams from *The Addams Family*.

Mom moved to Maine with a Southern accent, but it was teased out of her. Now she practices what is called the "Law of Conservation of R's" like all good Downeast-ahs. We typically remove the *r* from some words and add it to others. We say, "Sit right he-ay de-ah" and "I have an idear, let's go to Canader."

Accents aren't the only thing you will notice about a Downeast-ah; we also love our phrases. Sayings like "hard tellin' not knowin'" and "I'm tellin' you" and "yessah" and "dooryard" are common. "Right next door" refers to anything within a two-mile radius, whereas "a pretty good haul" means the destination is closer to two hours.

You might also notice a beat-up rusty pickup with two missing bumpers and a town name spray painted down the side like *Addison* or *Jonesport*. No, the owners are not busting with hometown pride, but, instead, taking advantage of the State's partial inspection law. It allows the use of vehicles that can only pass a partial inspection to continue to be used for fishing purposes, as long as the town name is displayed on the side.

My dad, Lyman Holmes, was born in Bangor and moved to Machias when he was in high school. His ancestors have worked as farmers, sailors, sail makers, lighthouse keepers, sardine packers, schoolteachers, carpenters, railroad workers, nurses, and lumbermen.

Dad still serves as a probate judge, is a local historian, and is a retired real estate attorney. He is a history buff and knows where most of our relatives are buried. During one visit to a cemetery in Harrington as a young man, he spied a headstone with the name "Christiannah" on it. He thought it was a pretty name and decided that if he ever had a daughter that would be her name. He was single at the time, but years later while they were dating, he told my mother his plan. She liked the name, too, which was good, considering he felt so strongly about it.

Some locals who hired my dad to write a real estate deed or handle other legal work, would pay him with crab meat, lobsters, or maple syrup. As probate judge, he handles matters such as name changes, adoptions, guardianships, and estate disputes. Everything is confidential, but he occasionally mentioned a classmate of mine and told me to make sure I was nice to them. He didn't say anything more and I didn't question him. I knew if he said it, it meant that kid was probably going through some tough times at home.

My parents were not sportsmen, but they loved nature. The closest Dad came to hunting was enjoying hunters' breakfasts. Dad loves all animals (except mice). If he found a spider in our house, he trapped it carefully using a glass cup, slipped a piece of paper between it and the wall, and released it outdoors. Even now, when we catch a fish, he handles it with the utmost care and apologizes to it before returning it to the water.

———————

My parents were nearly forty when I was born, which I found a bit embarrassing growing up. My friends' parents were much younger and just seemed more fun. Some of those parents coached my softball team, while mine just seemed old and strict and frugal.

But they came by it honestly. They were both raised by parents who survived the Great Depression, and that generation's sense of frugality remained strong in our household. Despite being comfortably middle class (they never hesitated to spend money on traveling to Disney, to Kentucky to visit family, or the Grand Canyon), they did not believe in unnecessary spending. We owned a dryer, but we never used it, except to store plastic bags. During the summer, we hung our clothes outside, and during the winter, we strung an indoor clothesline in the alcove off the kitchen. My mother claimed it added moisture to the air. We didn't use fabric softener, so I knew a towel was clean if it felt hard and scratchy. We were a one-car household. My parents shared a tan Buick LeSabre, but both walked to work unless the weather was bad. They valued being able to get six people into the car—their only prerequisite when it came to buying a vehicle.

The four of us each drank from a different colored cup—mine was pink and my brother's was green—and we rinsed and reused them for days until the dishwasher was fully loaded. Only then did we run it. Growing up frugally taught me more than to simply be careful with finances. It taught me patience, hard work and delayed gratification, traits that translate directly to hunting and fishing.

We didn't have an air conditioning unit because it rarely got hot in Machias. (It might get hot enough to wish for an air conditioning unit about three days each summer, but that was about it.) In our backyard, between the metal swing set and a spruce tree, under which my guinea pig was buried, we planted a garden to grow tomatoes,

Raking blueberries in Downeast Maine.

green beans, peas, cucumbers, and wildflowers. During winter, we kept the thermostat low, rarely setting it above sixty.

Overall, I think Downeast is a strong community. Because of our small population, limited resources, and harsh weather, we depend on our neighbors and help each other out in times of need. Baked bean suppers held at local churches are the social event of the month. Benefit suppers fill in the rest of the weekends, consisting of potlucks and silent auctions of goods donated by Shop 'n Save and True Value to benefit a family in need.

The people living in Washington County when I was growing up were highly independent. Everyone struggled with money; that was partly why everyone had so many side hustles. People sold fiddleheads and goose grass greens on the dike on the weekends. In May, when the alewives migrated and piled up at the large falls and dams in the area, locals like Bucket Davis scooped them up and sold them as lobster bait. Many folks raised their own animals and hunted and fished. We didn't have the population or finances to support expensive high school sports like hockey, tennis, or football. There were no ski mountains nearby. Ice skating was a community event. The Edwards family in Kennebec would clear their pond and invite the community over, offering hand-me-down ice skates from their three sons. Locals went tipping in the fall, breaking off limbs from balsam firs that are sold to Whitney's Wreaths who'd make wreaths sold to L.L.Bean and shipped across the country.

The Holmes family life was pretty routine for rural Maine. On Saturday mornings in the warmer months, we drove around and shopped at local yard sales. Since there were no clothing stores or big box stores, no Wal-Mart or The Home Depot, for example, we would cruise yard sales searching for what we needed. At a good Maine yard sale, you might find a moose antler, snowshoes, baby clothes, matchbox cars, old fishing equipment, puzzles, and lamps without bulbs, all displayed on fold-out tables or on blue tarps draped over the grass. I remember Mom buying us shoes and rollerblades at yard sales. It seemed that nearly everything we owned my mother bought from a yard sale—stuff borrowed from another person's life when they no longer needed those plates or that piece of furniture. We even bought a pet rabbit once. Sometimes a yard sale wouldn't cut it, so we took a trip to Bangor to the Goodwill store followed by grocery shopping at Sam's Club. We packed peanut butter and jelly sandwiches to eat along the way so we could save money.

From Machias, everything was a haul. The nearest movie theater was forty minutes away in Milbridge. This made dating difficult as a teenager. Add to this the fact that I was a head taller than all of the boys in my class. These were also the same boys that I attended school with since kindergarten; they all felt like annoying brothers to me, rather than potential love interests.

Finally, in eighth grade, one of those boys, Brian, rose to the challenge and asked me out to the movies. His mother drove us and she chaperoned from the back of the theater as we watched *Harry Potter and the Sorcerer's Stone*. The theater offered just one showing per day and the same movie ran for two weeks. Tickets cost $4.50, and if you paid with a five-dollar bill, you received a fifty-cent piece in change.

In high school, my first real boyfriend was Josh Kelley, a lobsterman from Beals Island who didn't finish high school. He was kind and hardworking and mechanically inclined (unlike my father). He eventually stopped coming over to our house because Mom always asked him to do work my father couldn't.

I spent summers working as his sternman, filling bait pockets on his open eighteen-foot fiberglass boat with an outboard named *White Lightning*. I designated a couple outfits as "bait outfits" since the smell of the rotten herring never washed out of my clothes. Given the size of the boat, he didn't really need a sternman and could easily handle all the work himself, but he humored me. We both loved it—"working" with a high school sweetheart out on the sea. We made good money for a couple of kids. His grandmother packed us crabmeat rolls for lunch, which they called dinner. To them, supper was the meal you ate in the evening, and they never ate "lunch." Josh's grandfather was a lobsterman, too, so his grandmother hand-picked crab meat for us and even for their cat, Wanderer. His fat body and shiny coat told me he ate well. It might sound absurd to feed your pet fresh, hand-picked crab meat, but to them it was

Fishing for mackerel.

just free cat food. I ate so many crab rolls during those summers that I refuse to eat them anymore.

Growing up, I was always tall and I was insecure about my height. In middle school photos, I was always stuck in the back row, a full head and shoulders taller than everyone in my class. In fourth grade, I tried pee-wee cheerleading, but being part of the base every time was boring, and I got a few bloody noses after being kneed in the face by the petite girl at the top of the pyramid. I decided to stick with basketball, where my height was an asset, and where I didn't have to worry about dropping someone from a great height.

I finally stopped growing as a freshman, topping out just shy of six feet, which was great for athletics but made buying pants and size 11 shoes difficult. I was scrawny. My basketball coach nicknamed me "Stick," which was better than other nicknames but not the description of a girl anyone would want to take to prom. I played center, and most of the other centers were slower than me, so I would often grab a defensive rebound and simply run to the other end of the court, shooting a layup over the small guard trying to defend me while the other center was still at half court. At our last home game my senior year, the cheerleaders made a sign, counting down to my one thousandth point. I needed thirty-one points and we were playing East Grand, the weakest team in the area, so it was doable. By the third quarter, we had a comfortable lead, so East Grand gave up trying to win and instead just tried to prevent me from reaching the milestone by double teaming me. They ended up fouling me a lot and I scored thirty-two points that game. Sports gave me confidence and I learned that, if I worked hard, I could excel.

I graduated with roughly the same thirty-four kids I had gone to school with since kindergarten. As a result, you get to know a lot about your classmates—which ones were spoiled by their parents, who got new cars, who got pregnant. Everyone knew everyone, and there were very few secrets. But that's just what it was like growing up in Downeast Maine.

Downeasters pride themselves on being independent, and we were, but every other family seemed to source their own food except for mine. I was interested in changing that—in doing more than tending a vegetable garden. Fishable water and hunting opportunities were all around me.

One summer day, my friend Whitney took me in her bathroom and showed me how to shave my legs. I watched enthralled as she slid the razor down her calf, so carefully and precisely. Later that afternoon, her dad drove us to a gravel pit and taught us to shoot his .30-06 rifle. We rolled up foam ear plugs and put them in our ears. I flinched the first time I squeezed the trigger, but after a couple tries, I hit the piece of paper. It didn't matter that we were girls; shooting was a life skill everyone should have. I remember the kick of the rifle against my shoulder, which hurt a little at first but didn't bother me. That was just a normal day, growing up Downeast, shaving our legs and shooting rifles!

2

A GIRL IN BOY SCOUTS

When I was six, I unofficially joined the Cub Scouts. Mom was an assistant leader for my older brother Martin's Cub Scout troop and, with Dad working overtime, I had nowhere else to go. Mom said I didn't have to participate, that I could just color or play quietly. But I wanted to do what the boys were doing. Once a month, we met at a local barn. We built butterfly houses and bird feeders, and we picked up trash. At the end of each meeting, I held my two fingers in a V and recited the Cub Scout pledge about doing my best, helping others, and obeying Cub Scout law. There were a dozen or so boys in the troop. They mostly ignored me and no one seemed to mind that I was part of the troop.

It was all fine and good until the Pinewood Derby. The Scout leader, Mr. Irving, was a skilled handyman and taught us how to sand and shape our cars to be aerodynamic. He explained that in a couple of months we would race them down a short ramp at the local elementary school against other troops. At our second meeting, I added stickers and my favorite number 24 to my car and attached wheels to it. At our third meeting, Mr. Irving and my mom taught

Martin and I at the Cub Scouts' Pinewood Derby.

us about mass and speed—meaning that a heavier car would go faster. That class the boys screwed small sheets of lead to the tops of their cars to increase the weight and speed. I didn't want to add metal to my car because it would look ugly, so I didn't.

When the night of the Pinewood Derby came, my brother and I carried our cars into a noisy gymnasium. Kids were running around, and people sat on the bleachers in front of a thirty-two-foot ramp.

As we walked to the registration table, my mother warned me: "Christi, they might not let you race yours because you're a girl." I shrugged, pretending not to care. But I was excited. I was proud of my car and wanted to see how fast it was.

"Martin Holmes," my brother told the man at the registration table and handed him his car for inspection. The man inspected the car to ensure it met the criteria and then looked for my brother's name on the clipboard in front of him.

"Troop 42 is right over there by the water fountain," the man said. "You'll go in about half an hour."

Martin and Mom walked over to join the rest of our troop.

"Christiannah Holmes," I said when it was my turn and held out my car for inspection.

He did not inspect my car and he did not look for my name on the list.

"I'm sorry sweetie, this is just for boys, but you can race your car down the ramp after everyone is done."

I nodded silently. But I was crushed.

I had worked hard on my car, just like everybody else. Why couldn't I race it? It's not like I was going to win anyway, because I didn't put those ugly weights on it.

"It's okay, Christi, when you're old enough to join Daisies, you'll do things that Martin isn't allowed to do," Dad said, trying to comfort me as I sulked toward the bleachers.

So I watched all the boys race their cars down the track. I watched excited kids collect their winning cars, all with metal plates. They advanced to the next round.

I mostly sat there confused and spinning the wheels on my car with my fingers. When the event ended, as promised, I got to race my car. Martin raced me and beat me every time (because of the lead), but it was still fun, and I was still proud of making my own derby car (one that wasn't ugly).

It was the accumulated experiences like this—being able to participate in something exciting, but not fully—that in some way motivated me, later on, to take full advantage of my opportunities, to dive into my passions without much thought about gender norms or expectations. I wanted, and still want, to be good at what I do, although the competition is no longer with Martin, or some imagined other, but usually with myself.

3
STALKING THE PERFECT CHRISTMAS TREE

"That one's not bad," said Martin as he pointed his mittened hand toward a small spruce tree. Mom broke a twig on the tree and smelled it.

"No, that is a spruce, we want a *balsam fir*," she said. "A Christmas tree." Although my parents were not sportsmen, they loved and appreciated nature and knew a thing or two about it. Mom wore a full-length L.L.Bean purple coat with coyote fur trim around the hood. It was her favorite winter coat—the one my father had given her the day I was born. She wore it everywhere.

"The first one we found was better anyway," I argued and wiped snot on the sleeve of my coat, a hand-me-down from my brother. It was spitting snow, just hard enough to make me put up my hood.

I was ten and, as we did every year, we were tromping around a forty-acre parcel of land we owned in Jonesport, looking for that year's

Christmas tree. Tall evergreens shaded the mossy woods. A narrow grass drive through the lot led to a secluded beach on Chandler Bay.

"Kids, come here!" Dad hollered as he pointed up into a birch tree. "A porcupine!"

We hurried over, our snowpants swishing with each step. "Isn't he cute?" my father asked us as he pulled a cumbersome pair of binoculars out of his backpack.

I stared in awe at the sleepy, unmoving creature twenty feet up. When it was my turn to look through the binoculars, I studied his quills. They were lighter in color than his face and his under fur, and the contrast reminded me of the older girls in school who highlighted their hair.

"I want to stay until he comes down," I announced. I wanted a better look. I wanted to see what the porcupine would do once it was back on the ground.

"As long as we are here, he won't come down," Dad said. "We have to leave him alone and give him space. Let's go to the beach for hot cocoa."

After a brief protest, I agreed. We bushwhacked through the crusty snow toward the sound of breaking waves. When we arrived, Martin and I searched for sea glass and threw rocks into the surf, while Mom produced a large Stanley thermos full of hot cocoa.

The wooded oceanfront land in Pobblestone Cove had been in our family since the 1850s, when my great-great-great-grandparents lived in Jonesport.

After our hot cocoa break, we left the beach and continued our tree search. As the day dragged on, *all* the trees started looking better and better. When we finally all agreed on one, Dad cut it down with a rusty hand saw and we dragged it to our old Buick and tied it to the roof with twine. Mom's frugal heart was happy, and my brother and I had compromised—the selected tree was neither of our first choices.

Here we are with our free range, wild Christmas tree.

On the drive, I wondered if the porcupine was still in his tree and envisioned our tree looking stunning inside our home. When we got home, we carried it gently into the house, leaving behind a trail of needles. In our living room, no longer surrounded by its peers, it looked a bit skinny and sparse. But we were proud of our tree, and once we decorated it, it appeared fuller and very festive. I was proud to be part of harvesting our own Christmas tree on family land.

4
HOOKED IN ALASKA

A
s my graduation from Machias Memorial High School neared, I didn't know what to study in college. I eventually decided to major in engineering for four reasons.

1. That's what Martin was studying.
2. I didn't hate math.
3. Since I was female and engineering was dominated by males, I might get some scholarships for being a minority.
4. Earning a degree in engineering wouldn't hurt regardless of what career I ultimately chose. It didn't seem so niche or specific that I would be pigeon-holed. I also told myself I could always switch majors if I didn't like it.

I was being practical.

I was accepted by other colleges, including Tufts and Dartmouth, but I chose the University of Maine and loved my time there. It helped that, unlike many other majors, engineering internships were paid. It helped even more that, as valedictorian at Machias, I received a full academic scholarship, so my tuition was covered. I was able to graduate debt free. Again, practical.

Although I loved Maine, I also had a hankering to travel. In 2009, during my junior year in college, I applied for a summer engineering internship with the National Park Service. I was accepted and soon received the news that I would be sent to either Seattle or Anchorage. I knew one person in each city, so I reached out to them both on Facebook to inquire about possible areas to avoid while renting, and to just give them a heads up that I might be in the area.

My friend James, who grew up in Maine, lived in Anchorage. We met while raking blueberries near my family camp. James was built like a linebacker, sporting big muscles but no discernible neck by the time he was sixteen. When he was fourteen, he had won a national title for bench press, and he attended private Dover Foxcroft Academy to pursue wrestling and football. After raking until ten in the morning on one sweltering day as teenagers, James invited a bunch of us to go swimming at his house on Meddybemps Lake, a large lake near the Canadian border known for its smallmouth bass. His parents weren't home, so James drove their pontoon boat. After a few laps, someone suggested we start tubing behind the boat, but James didn't have a tube. So, we went back to his house and scoured the property looking for something, anything, to use as a tube. We settled on a snow shovel and tried to ride that, but succeeded only in pantsing ourselves as we were dragged behind the boat.

After exchanging some messages with James, I grew excited about the prospect of working in Anchorage, so was disappointed when I ended up in Seattle. But since I had one week's vacation during my internship, and the flight was short, I decided to visit James anyway.

James took the week off and picked me up from the airport. I found Alaska a lot like Maine on steroids—more vast, bigger mountains, more remote wilderness, and more hunting and fishing opportunities. He was an avid angler, and since it was July, the sockeye salmon were running. I borrowed his roommate's waders and we fished every single day. It was my first true fishing experience. We saw stacks of zombie sockeye salmon, who had already spawned and were waiting for death. They wouldn't eat a lure or fly. The males had developed a prominent humpback and a sharp overbite, or kype, used to fight off other males. The skins of the dying fish had changed from silver to bright red and were the consistency of Jell-O. Their fins were worn down by digging nests in the gravel, and chunks were missing from their skin.

James owned a drift boat, so we packed it up with fishing and camping gear and put in on Kenai Lake, where the salmon were still edible. We fished the lake to its outlet—the Kenai River—and drifted down. We stopped on gravel bars and cast spinning gear, catching silvery, strong sockeyes. The daylight was long. We often fished until eleven at night and then woke up with the sun shining

My trip to Alaska was an eye opening experience.

into our tent at four in the morning. We had fresh salmon for dinner every night over a campfire. As we drifted, we saw moose and brown bears—and didn't fish in those areas. I trusted James and felt safe with him and his .44 Magnum. Alaska with James was the greatest adventure I'd ever been on.

Before this trip I thought I was outdoorsy, but only because I liked being outdoors and went on day hikes. But *this*—catching and eating our own food and sleeping outside, despite the threat of bears—I quickly realized, was *true* outdoorsy, and it was totally doable, with some preparation, knowledge, and guts. I loved it.

We pulled the drift boat out in Soldotna, a city near the Cook Inlet in the Kenai Peninsula Borough. It was roughly a three-hour drive to Anchorage. We drove back along scenic two-lane roads with mountains in the background, reminiscing about our trip and listening to Kenny Chesney on the radio. We played a game of who can spot the most moose; James won by spotting fourteen. Back in Anchorage, we stopped at a fish packing store and dropped my fish off—the store would freeze, vacuum seal, and package it for my flight the next day.

After a few days in the bush, returning to the city was jarring. Everyone was clean and everyone hurried. I needed a shower and a nap. The next day we picked up my nicely packaged salmon, and James drove me to the airport. I felt like I had been so far out of my routine, so disconnected from my normal life, and now I was suddenly back at a bustling airport with people coming and going and dragging suitcases behind them and saying goodbye to loved ones. I thanked James for the life-changing adventure as he offloaded my suitcase and boxes of fish onto the curb. We promised to see each other again soon, but deep down I wondered if that would happen. Then he drove away. I walked back into the airport, now with cell service and thinking about reentering the civilized world. I flew back to Seattle with boxes of fresh, bright orange sockeye salmon, my confidence soaring from this outdoor adventure.

5

TRAIL DEVA

As I approached Route 309 in Pennsylvania, my eyes lit up when I spied a cooler tucked beneath an oak. I was thru-hiking the Appalachian Trail and it had been three days since I had drank anything besides stream water. I craved a Gatorade or a soda, even a warm one.

Occasionally in places along the Appalachian Trail, "trail angels" leave treats or "trail magic." Sometimes you'll even find people set up flipping burgers on a grill. They might give you a Bible and invite you to their church, or give you a ride to town or even let you stay at their home. If they give you a small Bible, you'll politely accept it and thank them, then hike on. At the first shelter you arrive at a few miles down the trail, you'll find a pile of discarded Bibles.

I opened the cooler only to find empty Little Debbie boxes. Damn. Next to the cooler was a notebook tucked into a Ziploc bag. The last entry read, "Thanks for the snacks!" It was signed by Bear Bait and dated only a few hours earlier. I had just missed out. I marched on.

I didn't see any need to rush into a 9-to-5 career. I wasn't ready. I spent more than two years working seasonally before I got a full-time job. I waited tables at the Jordan Pond House, working on the lawn beneath The Bubbles in Acadia National Park. I traveled to Central America to study Spanish. I waited tables in the Virgin Islands. I spent four months backpacking in Europe.

And in the summer of 2011, I thru-hiked the Appalachian Trail.

The Appalachian Trail runs nearly 2,200 miles as it weaves through fourteen states between Springer Mountain in Georgia and Mount Katahdin in Maine. The Appalachian Trail Conservancy (ATC) says the Appalachian Trail is the world's longest hiking-only trail. The ATC estimates more than three thousand people attempt to hike the entire trail each year, but maybe a quarter of them succeed. In the first several decades the trail existed, women represented fifteen percent or fewer of those who completed the entire trail, but that percentage has grown steadily over the years, and women now represent more than a third of thru-hikers.

The trail is maintained by trail clubs and multiple partnerships and managed by the National Park Service, United States Forest Service, and the ATC. Most of the trail is in forest or wildlands, but some parts traverse towns, roads, and farms. From south to north it passes through Georgia, North Carolina, Tennessee, Virginia, West Virginia, Maryland, Pennsylvania, New Jersey, New York, Connecticut, Massachusetts, Vermont, New Hampshire, and Maine. Along the way, it also passes through six national parks, including the Great Smoky Mountains National Park, Blue Ridge Parkway, and Shenandoah National Park. Physically, the most difficult section to hike is in Maine and New Hampshire, but it's also the favorite of most hikers due to its remoteness.

When I told my parents my plan, they were nervous but supportive. Dad bought me a SPOT GPS emergency tracking device with an SOS button that worked on a satellite and automatically sent my coordinates to a 911 dispatcher if I pressed it. Mom read a book about thru-hiking which eased her fears. She knew that adventures should be pursued; in fact, she rode a motorcycle around Europe as a young adult.

I was determined to succeed. I went to L.L.Bean with a credit card to buy all the gear I thought I needed and then headed south to Georgia. I was twenty-three-years-old and on March 20, I began hiking the trail back to Maine alone. I was a year out of college with a love of the outdoors. I figured if I could accomplish the trail, there wasn't much I couldn't do outdoors.

It's easy to get romantic about hiking the trail—getting away from the hustle and bustle and "finding yourself" as they say. In reality, toward the end of the five months of walking, some days felt like the movie *Groundhog Day*—I was just reliving the same day over and over and over. I knew that wasn't true, that I was making my way north and crossing new terrain each day, but the endless forests and the ups and downs and the sore legs and sore feet made the journey feel endless. It honestly became difficult to differentiate one day from the next. I nearly hit the wall in New Hampshire, but pushed through to Katahdin, arriving there in August.

Don't get me wrong, I met many wonderful people on the trail. I felt safe and felt absolute freedom. I never felt threatened by passersby, and most everyone I met was affable and respectful and I gained confidence in myself, but the hike is *not* as romantic as some make it sound. You literally just wake up and walk.

Every.

Single.

Day.

You fantasize about scrambled eggs and hashbrowns, a cup of hot chocolate, or chocolate of any kind, for that matter, or a hot shower and a massage. In reality, you just wake up, and you walk.

I was usually walking through a forest that might open up to offer one or two nice views per day. And then some days I dodged traffic while running across a major highway. Some nights I heard traffic while bedding down at the campsite. Although in some ways these familiar sounds comforted me, I also knew they did not signify I was nearing any end, so I grew to resent those noises of civilization. I found myself more at peace away from roads, surrounded only by natural sights and sounds.

While walking the trail, most people get blisters on their feet, welted-up, itchy as hell mosquito bites, and sunburns that peel in chunks. They might hike in wet shoes for four days straight, which causes more blisters—the painful, in between your toes type of blisters. You eat the same food almost every day, you're cold, you miss your friends, you yearn for a good conversation, a lazy day around the house, a hot shower, and a warm, dry bed. All of these things happened to me.

I think more people fail to finish the hike due to the psychological grind than the actual physical toll. Despite the hardships, your body gets used to the physical demands in a couple of weeks. I know mine did. But mentally, the monotony and the daily grind can be hard.

I wasn't much of a hiker before I started out on the trail. Yes, I'd taken some day hikes, but never truly went overnight backpacking. As I usually do, I began to dig in. To prepare myself mentally, I read firsthand accounts from women who had thru-hiked. You get used to having sore muscles and swollen feet, but it's the mental grind of hiking in a wet, green tunnel all day every day that causes people to quit.

Also, luckily for me, the trail comes upon an Appalachian Trail outfitter shop the third day out and the staff will help overhaul your gear to let you know what you *really* need. Staff emptied the contents of my backpack on the floor and I ended up mailing one-third of my stuff home to lighten the load. Some hikers went so far as to cut their toothbrushes in half to shed pounds. It was common to see hikers in raincoats and rain pants in eighty-degree weather while doing laundry—because we didn't pack a change of clothes. I wore the same shirt, a black tank top, the entire two thousand mile hike. I smelled delightful.

The staff at the Georgia outfitters also advised me to buy sneakers two sizes too big to help prevent blisters. I took their advice. I ended up wearing out four pairs of Brooks running shoes, which were comfortable enough for my twenty-five-mile days on what is, generally, a well-maintained trail. The too-big shoes trick worked, because I didn't get my first blister until I was a thousand miles into my hike.

Most mornings I woke up with the sun and listened to the birds chirping the forest awake around five-thirty. I quickly packed up my gear and started hiking. I snacked on apples and granola bars, occasionally took a break to snap a photo, sign a shelter log, filter water, or use a privy.

I usually hiked until about six each night or until I found a shelter. There are three-sided shelters located about every eight miles, and they all have water nearby and you can meet other hikers for some company—I never spent a night alone. I cooked a rice or pasta Knorr side for dinner, wrote in my journal, and was asleep by nine (if no one was snoring).

I once heard about a thru-hiker who woke up, smoked some pot, and accidentally hiked eight miles *south* before realizing he was going the wrong way. He turned around, hiked back those eight miles north, and slept in the same shelter as the previous night, resulting in a sixteen-mile "zero day" (a day you go zero miles, usually a rest day, in town).

All thru-hikers go by a trail name or else there would be too many Matts and Mikes. My trail name was Deva, named after the model of Gregory backpack I had (I later upgraded to a Hyperlite Mountain Gear pack made in Biddeford) and the fact that I shaved my legs every four days, which, compared to most thru-hikers, elevated me to diva status. Every four days or so, the trail would run near or through a town and I'd hitchhike in and do my laundry, split a motel room with other hikers, and take a shower (and shave). I would eat big meals until I felt sick.

I hiked about half of my journey with two middle-aged men from New York— Porter, so named because he portaged his wife's gear and liked porter beers, and Pace, who always went first and set the pace. He also had a pacemaker. Because of his pacemaker, he ran under transmission lines so that the electricity didn't cause his pacemaker to get out of beat.

Other people I met on the trail, included: Timber because he once knocked down a tree while attempting to hang his bear bag; Bear Bait because his food was stolen by a hungry black bear; Spike because he hiked all day carrying a railroad spike another hiker had snuck in his pack as a joke; Click who was a photographer who carried a DSLR; Captain Planet who picked up trash along the trail; Caboose because she always hiked in the back of the group; and Calf who had *huge* calves.

On Memorial Day weekend, more than two months into my walk, I decided to leave the trail and visit my brother, Martin, in Washington, D.C., just a short train ride from Harpers Ferry, Virginia. Harpers Ferry is often considered the half-way point of the trail—many people stop and get their photo taken at the ATC. I was the 212th thru-hiker of the year, so far. Once I reached D.C., Martin and I partied on his rooftop apartment, played beer pong, went out clubbing, and sang karaoke. It was a nice break, a needed change of pace, but it felt weird going from the quiet and peacefulness of the trail to a club throbbing with music. I had gotten used to having similar conversations every day with people doing the exact same thing I was doing—and suddenly, here I was in a big city, the nation's capital, awkwardly chatting with people. I literally didn't know what to talk about. I had managed to remove myself from current events and seemingly talked only about food and gear for months. I didn't have any cute clothes to wear, which made me self-conscious. But, after weeks of waking up early to get back on the trail, sleeping in after a long night out on the town felt luxurious. Even so, by the end of the weekend, I was ready to return to the trail. We said our goodbyes and I boarded the train back to Harpers Ferry to resume my long march north.

After my detour, Porter and Pace had gotten pretty far out ahead of me. For my first two days back, in an effort to catch up with my trail friends, I hiked sixty miles. I think they might have also slowed down a bit, too, which helped me, and I caught up with them one evening at a shelter. It was good to see them again and I regaled them with stories about my foray into the nation's capital with Martin.

Hiking through the Smoky Mountains in March was cold, but walking through Virginia in June was hot, and July in Pennsylvania was even hotter. Just brutal. I started out with a twenty degree sleeping bag, but eventually bought a lighter sleeping bag and mailed my heavier one home. Despite my degree in engineering, I wasn't much for converting the temperature rating from Celsius to Fahrenheit on the German-made sleeping bag I bought, so my first few nights were *cold*.

One night I woke up so cold that I asked another hiker to snuggle with me. After that, the hiker, Crop Duster, texted me whenever the forecast called for cooler weather and would ask if I needed a snuggle buddy. Yes, he was dubbed Crop Duster for being gassy and thus always hiked in the back of the group. Fortunately for me, I hiked faster than he did and eventually the evenings warmed up.

When I crossed into Maine, my parents came to meet me and brought a spread of food. After hiking twelve-hour days carrying a twenty-pound pack, I could eat it all. I mean, I often dreamed about food. I ate entire pizzas, half gallons of ice cream, hot dogs, and always got dessert.

Food was discussed daily among hikers. "What's the most caloric dense food?" was a topic one evening. After weeks on the trail, we were all getting sick of eating the same foods day after day and agreed that butter was probably the answer. It wasn't too practical to carry butter in the summer and it didn't taste good on its own so I opted for entire packages of Oreos and Fritos since they don't crush as easily as other chips.

Hikers also liked to discuss, often to death, pace and gear. Everyone asks what day you started, and believed faster hikers obviously needed to slow down and enjoy the trail more. The gear debate was never ending. Inflatable sleeping pad or foam? Water filter, SteriPEN, iodine tablets, or unfiltered? Stove or no stove? Tent or hammock? It was tiresome.

I didn't have a smart phone back in 2011, so I carried a cell phone, camera, SPOT GPS emergency device, and iPod touch to access the internet via Wi-Fi when I was in a town. We were so detached from society that I remember reading in a trail journal that Osama Bin Laden had been killed.

In a way, taking on such a major physical feat made me lazy, or maybe extremely efficient. A sign pointing down a side trail reading EXCELLENT VIEWS FOUR HUNDRED FEET was quickly dismissed. I thought, *I have 2,181 miles to walk, no way I'm going to walk an optional extra eight hundred feet.* And I felt a highly rated shelter that was less than a quarter mile off the trail was a definite no go.

Despite my ironic laziness, I reached the summit of Katahdin to complete my thru hike in August, and Katahdin was by far the hardest day of hiking. I spent all day climbing this one mountain. That morning, I had met up with my parents below tree line, along the iconic Hunt Trail. We started early, before the other AT hikers because I knew I would have to hike more slowly with my parents as company. When we reached the iron rungs, my parents said, "Well, this is good for us," and they stopped there. They were sixty at the time and weren't used to hiking tall mountains in a day. Once they turned back, I resumed my preferred pace. I was in such good shape that it felt good to get back up to speed. The other hikers finishing that day had passed me earlier on and I hustled to catch up to them.

The day I finished my thru hike of the Appalachian Trail.

When I got to Tableland, a wide, flat, exposed area with grass and rocks a short way from the actual summit, I noticed the other thru-hikers, like Clifford in his red shirt, and Smurf, and Moose, and

Baby, were sitting down having a snack. I realized that they didn't really need a break there. I don't recall if anyone said it aloud, but there was a definite sense that we were about to complete something incredible. Many of these individuals were still high school kids who had been out there longer than me, and they were all friends. To be honest, I didn't want to summit alone. When we got to the sign marking the summit, at 5,267 feet, many in the group were emotional. I felt happy and proud, but also ready by that point to move on to the next chapter—the next adventure.

In hindsight, the best part of the experience was what, at the time, seemed like the worst—the simplicity. There was no rent due, no car to register, no dentist appointments. Nothing. No temptation to keep up on the latest trends. My daily to-do list, which now is endless, was so simple—walk north.

6

SALTY AND SUNBURNED IN THE VIRGIN ISLANDS

W hen I was about twelve, my friend Kelsey invited me to St. Croix in the U.S. Virgin Islands with her and her dad. It was a great adventure, riding around on the left hand side of the road, squeezing into the back seat of an antique Land Rover, and snorkeling in the cobalt blue sea. When I was in college, we planned our own trip, and this time we booked a tent site at a campground on the beach on St. John. We swam and snorkeled during the day, and hitchhiked into town, where we sang karaoke at night. We thought: *Wouldn't it be awesome to live here?*

So, in 2012, after hiking the Appalachian Trail, I did just that. I convinced three friends to move with me, and we booked a tent site—at the same campground Kelsey and I stayed at years prior— while searching for an apartment to rent. The four of us eventually crammed into a small, two-bedroom apartment that we rented for two thousand dollars a month. I applied at every restaurant in town

Fishing for mahi on St. John.

and got hired as a hostess, then waitress, at Morgan's Mango, an outdoor Caribbean Seafood place with a tree house vibe.

The restaurant bought fresh fish and Caribbean lobster from local West Indian fishermen. For my birthday, I begged one of the fishermen to let me fish with him and his crew. He reluctantly agreed and told me to meet him the next morning at seven at the docks. He finally arrived at nine (this is called *being on island time,* the thought being there is no reason to rush) and we, along with his two boys, piled into his sixteen-foot boat and headed out to sea.

My butt quickly grew numb as it bounced on the hard seat, the sea soaking me every time we hit a wave. I held onto a rope. I noticed the island of St. John growing smaller and smaller at just about the same time I noticed we didn't have any life jackets on board. The captain and boys spoke in their native language while scanning the horizon and pointing toward some circling sea birds. He increased speed and we raced over to their location. As we got closer, I noticed flying fish soaring above the sea for fifteen feet or so before dipping back in. The boys baited small live fish onto a hook and threw them toward the flying fish. They didn't have fishing rods, just a line on a large spool. Almost immediately one of the lines grew tight and I watched a blueish green mahi jump into the air. The boy wrapped the line back onto the spool quickly by hand and brought the fish into the boat. On board, the fish changed color, losing all its blue and becoming a greenish-gray as it died. All three men were handlining mahi while I watched in awe at the organized chaos of bait, mahi, and hooks thrashing in the boat.

Then it stopped. And we drove around looking for birds, and for more flying fish, and we repeated the chaos.

This went on for hours and I eventually felt confident enough to try it. We only had two gloves total among the four of us, so the line dug into my hands as I brought mahi after mahi aboard the boat. At one point, I had to pee. When I told the captain, he told me to jump overboard and they would help me back in the boat. Not wanting to complain or seem like a high-maintenance American, I jumped overboard without a lifejacket, miles and miles offshore, trusting these strangers. They helped me back in.

We fished into the late afternoon. I had no idea we would fish all day, and given our late start, I was hungry and thirsty. One of the boys gave me a Coke. Finally, with our holds full of mahi, we headed back to the island. At the docks, we unloaded our catch. I was sunburnt and starving, my lips cracked, and my hair, body, and clothes were covered with dried sea salt, and I was smiling from ear to ear.

Morgan's Mango only opened for dinner, which left me my days to explore the beautiful island as much as I could afford financially. I didn't have a car, so I either tried to hitchhike or took a taxi to the beach or the hiking trails.

I don't regret living on St. John for six months, but it certainly wasn't the island life that I expected. It is hard to afford to live there. Because it is an island, all goods must be imported, making them costly. For example, a small jar of peanut butter was seven dollars (and remember, this was 2012). And because St. John is a tourist destination, beach fees, taxis, and rental boats were priced accordingly. I ate a lot of the free rice and beans that Morgan's Mango offered to its employees. And my roommates and I occasionally worked up enough courage to sneak into the Westin Resort so we could sit by their pool on our day off. Most of the locals spent their free time partying at night, but I wasn't interested in that. I was glad for the experience, but by the end I was ready to go back home to Maine.

7
ARGOS

All I had ever wanted since I was a little girl was to own a dog. My dad is allergic to them, so we never had a dog or cat growing up. I was allowed to get a guinea pig, which I named Buttercup.

By January 2014, I was living in Machias and working for CES, a small civil engineering firm, doing surveying and designing subdivisions. My six months in the Virgin Islands turned out to be my last pre-job adventure. I was now in my mid-twenties and I was growing restless living in Washington County, still living in the same small, rural town where I grew up. I wanted to move to Southern Maine, which meant I needed to quit my job. I felt this would be a perfect time to get a puppy, so I started planning. I researched how to choose the best breed for my lifestyle and found a quiz from Animal Planet that asked multiple-choice questions such as:

What size dog do you want?

How much grooming are you prepared to do (i.e., Do you want a long-haired or short-haired dog)?

How much time can you spend exercising your dog per day?

Do you want a dog for protection?

How trainable do you want your dog to be?

Do you live in a particularly hot or cold climate?

I matched 100 percent with a Brittany, no second-place matches. I was familiar with Brittanys, since my friend, Kelsey, had two of them. I adored her two dogs, Alex and Jake. They were athletic and agile, sweet, smart, and only forty pounds, so not too big. Although I wasn't looking for a hunting dog specifically, it didn't hurt that they were bred for upland hunting, which in Maine means partridge and woodcock.

Previously known as Brittany spaniels, the spaniel was dropped from their name in 1984, since they have the traits of a pointer, not a spaniel, which are flushing dogs. They were named for the province in France where they originated.

Next, I searched for a Brittany breeder in Maine and inquired about any upcoming litters. I emailed a breeder who put me in contact with Bo and Christine Longley in Litchfield, who planned to have a litter in three months. I met them and their pack of Brittanys at their home. Brandy greeted me, the female they planned on breeding, as well as Brandy's father, grandmother, and great-grandmother. The Longleys bragged about each dog and shared photos as proud parents do their children. These were not only excellent hunting dogs but family dogs that took up space in the bed and hearts of the Longleys. I wrote a check for a deposit.

In the meantime, I bought supplies, researched puppy play classes, and went to the library for training suggestions. I took notes like I was studying for the SATs. I checked out *The Art of Raising a Puppy* and books by The Dog Whisperer, Cesar Milan.

The entire process didn't feel real until the late March day when Argos and his littermates were born. Bo sent me a photo of Brandy under a heat lamp. She was panting, which resembled a smile, as her six newborn puppies were squeezed together on top of each other nursing. Because I had put my deposit down so early, I had second pick of the litter behind the Longleys who were keeping one puppy for themselves. When the puppies were four weeks old, I finally got to visit them. I sat on the floor as they crawled around, but mostly they slept. When they were six weeks old, we went outside together. They chewed on my shoelaces and chased the wing of a partridge. They were all so sweet and fun. I chose Argos because I wanted a male and because he had the most brown spots. The other male littermates were nearly all white.

I brought Argos home with a blue whale blanket and a stuffed hedgehog toy. The breeder said the scent of his family on the toy and blanket would make the transition easier for him. He slept in the passenger seat on my drive home. I took him for a long walk when we arrived at his new home, something I saw recommended in a book. He trotted confidently with his ears perked and stopped to investigate every mud puddle and tried to pick up every stick he found along the dirt road. He slept in a crate with his whale blanket and hedgehog next to my bed, fairly content knowing I was nearby. But in the mornings, at the slightest sign of me stirring, he began pawing and whining to be let out.

When Argos was four months old, we went to an upland dog hunting training day hosted by the Central Maine Brittany Club. A quail was planted in the tall grass, and when it was Argos' turn, he ran around a bit, then slowed and tentatively crept toward it. He stopped with his front paw lifted. The bird burst into flight while Argos watched in shock. We celebrated his first point and his first bird by rolling around in the grass together.

Back home, I tied a partridge wing to a string on a stick and encouraged Argos to point it. I repeated the word *bird* as he pointed and I wriggled the wing around. He rang a bell next to the door when he needed to go out, although he took advantage of this and rang it constantly, regardless of whether he needed to do his business. He learned his name and stared hard into my eyes, trying to decipher what I was thinking and wanted from him.

We took three walks a day and worked on *heel, stay,* and *come.* He loved our off-leash hikes in the woods where he ran circles around me. Inside, he sat by the window patiently for hours, watching for squirrels and birds. I banged two-by-fours and played audio clips of thunder and fireworks on my laptop while he ate dinner to get him used to loud noises. I bought a blank gun and slowly conditioned him to the sound of gunshots. That summer we attended an AKC Upland Hunt Test in Kennebunkport, where Argos gained exposure to chukars (training birds) and I asked questions about training from the other more experienced owners.

Argos was seven months old by the fall's hunting season. One weekend in October, I took him partridge hunting up to my friend April's camp near Houlton. There was no road to her camp, just a four-wheeler trail. We rode into her camp, and then walked the woods, following Argos. Neither April nor I had ever hunted over a dog, and Argos had never hunted, so we were all learning. Argos' bell jingled, while I repeated, every few minutes, "Find the bird." He flushed many birds, too far from the reach of April's or my 20-gauges.

When trying something new, immediate success appeals to many people. If they don't find it, they grow discouraged and abandon a potential hobby. Someone new to fishing, who doesn't have any success, will likely give it up. The same is true for hunting. Experiencing at least some success early is extremely motivating. The first time I went fly fishing I caught a small brook trout on a dry fly, and it immediately became a hobby I wanted to pursue. But if success is measured by harvesting an animal, Argos and I didn't succeed during our entire first season upland hunting. However, I quickly realized that everything I did with Argos was a success. I just had to change my metric. If we came home from a hunt empty-handed, well, I still took my best friend on a long, off-leash walk. Those were good days.

By the following fall, I was determined to get Argos a bird. I trained him during the off season and he passed four hunt tests, making him an AKC Junior Hunter. If we didn't get a bird this

Argos was my best friend and we learned to hunt together. *Photo by Cait Bourgault*

year it would be solely my fault. The bell on Argos' collar jingled when he jumped out of my car at a pheasant release site in Saco, down the road from where we lived. My friend and avid upland hunter Landon joined us. The State stocked pheasants here, so we were confident we would find some action. Argos ran fast and far through the tall, wet grass along the pole line. *Too fast and too far,* I thought, as Landon and I walked quickly over uneven ground, trying and failing to keep up. Ahead, Argos bumped a hen pheasant out of the grass and into the sky some fifty yards ahead of us. She flew into the woods. Argos took one jump and stopped and looked back toward me.

"Ok, well now that that's out of his system and he knows what's going on here, maybe he'll settle down and point them instead of flushing them," I explained to Landon. I told Argos to "find the bird" and he went back to running around like a madman.

I watched Argos' every move, searching for any changes to speed. Like playing Red Light, Green Light in eighth grade gym class, Argos abruptly froze and twisted his body. I interpreted his posture to mean business. When he was on point with a slow tag wag and eye contact with me, it meant he was unsure. But this was a hard point, his tail quivered with anticipation and his eyes locked on a bush. I had seen this pose during our hunt tests, and learned not to trust where he was looking, but realized that this was the moment he picked up the scent. The bird may be twenty yards upwind of him, or inches from his face. Landon and I flanked both sides of Argos. Landon volunteered to try flushing the bird for me. I repeated the word "woah" as my heart pounded. Landon walked slowly ahead of Argos, kicking his feet in large sweeps, until a male pheasant erupted from the bushes. The bird flew directly in front of me and I dropped it with my second shot. Argos ran to the bird, bit it once, then sprawled out in the grass beside it, his back legs spread like a frog, panting and looking up at me. It's like watching a synchronized dance, watching him do what he was born to do with centuries of breeding rooted deep within his DNA. The three of us hooted and hollered. I placed our first bird in Landon's vest and we went off to find more.

Why can't every month be October? I wondered.

8
TRACKING A BUCK

I sat twenty feet high in a hang on stand in a spruce tree, over-looking a small bog the size of a basketball court in Pownal. It was the second week of November, and last week's snow blanketed the ground. It was hard and crunchy and with no wind blowing; I would hear anything walking nearby. It was nearly silent except for the occasional rumble of a car driving half a mile away. It was too cold on my fingertips to scroll on my phone, which was good because I shouldn't do that anyways. I had to stay focused for a few more hours.

"These are the most important hours," I coached myself. "It only takes a second for a deer to come by."

I was bundled in men's wool pants and a down jacket, hands tucked into a muff at my waist, my Remington .308 resting across my lap. A squirrel scurried back and forth, up and over a log, readying its stash for winter. I wondered whether he carried acorns or mushrooms.

By this time in my hunting career, I was used to sitting for hours and seeing nothing. I had started deer hunting six years earlier and I hadn't shot a deer yet. In fact, I rarely even *saw* a deer. As the afternoon waned, I checked my watch—two-thirty. Two hours until legal hunting time ended. I told myself I could eat a snack at four, which gave me something to look forward to and something to do when the time came. I watched that busy squirrel scurry by again.

Deer hunting tested my ability to withstand boredom. In today's world, most of us are seldom bored. In line at the grocery store? Text a friend or watch a funny video on your phone. We are not comfortable being bored, with being alone with our thoughts, with listening to our inner monologue. When hunting deer, you must fight sheer boredom for hours and hours and remain totally present. If you move too much, you'll spook deer before you even see them. If you're looking at your phone, the only buck of the day might walk by silently without you even noticing.

I took the Primos doe call out of my vest pocket and turned it over, counted to ten, and turned it over again. It was a "can call" with holes on both sides. It let out a soft bleat each time I turned it, imitating a doe in heat. I watched the squirrel make another trip over the log.

At four o'clock sharp I cautiously unzipped my camo waist pack and removed a package of six small peanut butter crackers. I put one in my mouth and chewed. The chewing was loud inside my head. Then I heard something. *Probably another squirrel*, I thought. The noise came from behind me, over my left shoulder, but didn't sound close. I took the deer call out again and turned it over, just in case. I craned my neck and peered into the forest. Nothing. I put another cracker in my mouth.

Then movement caught my eye. It probably was not a deer, and if it was, it was probably a doe. I didn't have a doe tag for this zone.

Then I saw brown.

It *was* a deer! But was it a buck? The brown sauntered toward me as the unchewed cracker sat in my mouth.

Antlers!

A buck!

I didn't count the points or study the rack, but just seeing antlers was enough for me. I raised my gun up and steadied the deer in my scope. I had a hard time finding him and keeping him in my scope.

Breath in.

Breath out.

I clicked the safety off.

Breath in.

Breath out.

About eighty yards. If he turns, shoot, my inner dialogue coached.

He turned.

I shot.

The squirrel was gone and so was my cracker, although I don't remember eating it.

Did I hit him?

My hands were shaking.

Through my scope I spied blood in the snow where the deer had been standing. I took out my phone and texted my friend, Randy, who was working nearby. I was sitting in his tree stand.

He must have these deer on payroll, I chuckled to myself.

Randy is a flannel-wearing burly guy in his fifties with a long, grayish beard who works as a nuisance trapper and Registered Maine Guide. When he arrived, we walked to the spot where the deer had stood. Randy crouched down and studied the blood-stained snow, "There's a lot of blood, but blood looks bigger in snow, so hard to tell how good it's hit."

We followed the blood trail through the woods. We marked our way with orange flagging tape every few feet. I was positive we would find the deer crumpled up just around the next corner. That's how deer hunting works, right? We kept walking.

We followed the blood trail for fifteen minutes or so until it was completely dark. The deer was still going. He had bedded down once, and we studied the pool of blood. It was red, with no green or brown material, which would have indicated a gut shot, but I must not have hit his heart or lungs either since the deer was still alive. We didn't see any drag marks in the snow, so his legs were okay. We decided to back out and wait a couple of hours, hoping the deer would succumb to his injuries.

My stomach was in knots, but I remained confident we would find him; there was just too much blood not to.

I called Scot Clontz, one of the State's certified tracking dog handlers. He said he could meet me in the morning.

"Promise me you won't go back after that deer tonight, you'll just spread the blood around," Scot said, "increasing the chances of a coyote crossing its path, and you will make my job harder in the morning."

"I promise," I said.

I lied.

Randy insisted we not leave the deer out overnight given the number of coyotes in the area, and I trusted Randy's guidance. At about nine, with fresh batteries in our headlamps, we began tracking the deer again. The night was moonless, dark, and chilly. We easily followed the blood trail through the snow-covered woods, but out in the fields where the ground had less or no snow, we struggled to find blood.

Once, we bumped the buck and heard him cross a small stream ahead of us. We backed out again, and hoped he would bed down and expire. At midnight, we went in again, and that's when we saw it—a drag mark in the snow. I had shot the deer in the leg.

I felt terrible. I knew this animal was suffering and struggling. A major reason I started hunting was to mitigate animal suffering, and now look at what I had done. This was *not* how I envisioned it. I was ashamed and disappointed in myself. And what would we do if we caught up to it? It wasn't going to bleed out from a leg wound that night. We couldn't legally shoot it again because it was nighttime. At one in the morning, we decided to go home and wait for Scot. I would not tell him what we had done.

I tossed and turned in bed. Sleep evaded me, like the buck I injured. I thought through the possible scenarios that awaited us come daylight.

What if we don't find him?

What if coyotes find him first?

I remembered an audio recording I once heard of a deer crying as coyotes ate it alive. Here I am, in my warm bed, and coyotes could be eating my buck alive at this very moment. *What have I done?* Six years I've been trying to get a deer. I finally get my chance. And I fail. I should have given up on deer hunting, stuck to turkey and duck hunting.

No, that's not true, deep down I knew the reason I never gave up on deer hunting—I am not a quitter. And I certainly wasn't going to quit now. I hate to quit and I hate to fail.

I met Randy the next morning and we anxiously waited for Scot to arrive. Scot pulled up in an old Corolla, wearing jeans and sneakers, despite the snow. Scot was a middle-aged man who looked a bit unprepared, but I put a lot of faith in him and his abilities. He carried his beagle, Darwin, under his arm.

"Darwin and I will go first," he said. "And if the deer is alive, you do not shoot until I give you the go ahead."

Scot put Darwin down where we had stopped tracking the night before. I was impressed to watch Darwin work, to say the least. He spent a few minutes sniffing and turning and deciphering which direction the deer went, and then he was off, pulling at the leash, trying to break free and run. I struggled to keep up, at times jogging with my 12-gauge and chambered slug over my shoulder. Unlike my rifle, which I only fired a couple times a year, I was more comfortable handling and aiming my 12-gauge, since I used it frequently for bird hunting. Part of me wondered if the scope on my rifle was off.

About ten minutes into the track, Darwin started howling. "We must be close," Scot translated. At the edge of a stream, Darwin stopped to work out which direction the deer had gone. I heard ice breaking and looked upstream. I watched a buck struggle across the barely iced-over river. He slipped and broke through, but made it to the other side.

"There he is!" I exclaimed as the buck limped into the forest on the opposite bank. Scot scooped up Darwin and we crossed a beaver dam nearby. We walked upstream, found fresh blood, and Scot put Darwin back to work.

The woods were denser on this side of the stream, but almost immediately we jumped the deer. He disappeared through the thickets and I didn't have a shot. Darwin tracked him back toward the stream and we caught up to him in the open. The buck was in a clearing along the stream's edge about thirty yards away. He was still moving, limping away from us.

Scot gave me the go ahead.

I put the gun's bead on the buck's neck and fired.

The deer dropped.

We walked over to the buck, my first deer. A medium-size eight pointer. Randy patted me on the back and congratulated me. I thanked him and Scot profusely. I knelt behind the buck and sank my fingers into his thick, oatmeal-colored coat. His rear leg dangled from his body. I shook my head in disbelief—what resiliency, what strength—to keep going so long on three legs.

I sat with the buck for a few minutes until it was time to field dress him. I was relieved that this buck was no longer suffering. *This* had been my goal all along, back when I shot that first spruce grouse. I had hoped for this, unsure if I would ever achieve it. The highs and lows from the past sixteen hours flooded out in tears of shame and sorrow, appreciation and pride.

I gutted the buck with Randy's guidance, while he studied his phone to determine the easiest way out. To get to the closest road,

I had to call in a tracking dog to help find my first deer. Darwin the beagle found him very quickly.

we would have to drag the deer past a house. Randy rigged up a stick for leverage and he and Scot dragged the buck headfirst toward the road. Once in sight of the house, Randy knocked on the door and asked if we could drag the deer across their lawn to the road; they agreed. This was my first time dragging a buck. I tried by myself and thought, *There's no way I could ever do this alone.* I was glad to have their help.

Hunting whitetails in Maine has taught me a lot about myself. Sitting in a tree stand for hours, cold, hungry, bored, and discouraged humbled me and taught me patience. Alarms at four in the morning taught me discipline. Tracking my first deer for hours taught me perseverance. But the most important lessons I have learned deer hunting are to slow down, stay in the moment, and never give up.

9
BROOKIES IN BAXTER

In 2015, I was living in Southern Maine working as a civil engineer and I was dating a guy named Nick. He was thin, balding, and barely taller than me, which made me wonder if I weighed more than him. I didn't like the thought of that. Nick and I met online. He was impressed that I had hiked the entire Appalachian Trail. I liked that he was impressed by my accomplishments. He was a quiet, studious type of guy so I had to do most of the talking.

After a couple of weeks of hanging out, we decided to drive twenty miles up the coast to Freeport to L.L.Bean's flagship store. Nick held the store's fly rod motif door handle for me as I entered. The doors didn't have locks, because the place is open 24 hours a day. We strolled past the hunting section, climbed the stairs, and walked past the conventional fishing gear until we reached the fly fishing department. I had never been fly fishing. Nick explained rod weights and lengths and floating versus sinking line, and we both ogled the hundreds of flies in their display cases, organized by color and size. The flies reminded me of colorful beads in a bracelet making kit I had in middle school, except these flies were beautiful on their own, not just as part of a bigger project.

Despite a financially healthy career as a merchant mariner, Nick fretted over the price of a new fly rod. He wanted to get into fly fishing for striped bass, so he needed a big rod that could withstand the salt and launch heavy flies out into the surf. After a lot of back and forth with the sales associate, Nick chose a nine-foot-long 9-weight L.L.Bean rod and reel. He seemed happy. On the drive back south, he invited me to his family's camp located near Mount Katahdin the following weekend. From their camp near Baxter State Park, we could hike into his favorite remote pond and fly fish for rising trout at sunset. It all sounded pretty romantic. I was in.

I left work early on Friday, and we drove three hours north in Nick's dented Chevy pickup. About two hundred miles north of Portland, we took the exit for Millinocket. Not far from the exit, we saw a young bull moose standing on the shoulder of the road. To my dismay, Nick hit the gas and swerved toward the moose, driving up alongside it while it galloped for a few seconds before ducking into the woods. My instinct when I saw a moose was to slow down to avoid a potential collision, and hopefully snap a photo. Since Nick grew up here, he saw moose as often as I saw squirrels and he was comfortable playing chicken with them. We laughed about it.

We drove by a long-shuttered paper mill. Millinocket was once known as Magic City because of the way it sprouted almost fully formed in the wilderness to become a thriving paper mill town. The mill eventually declined and closed, the town struggled, and now Millinocket is known mostly as the gateway to Mount Katahdin and Baxter State Park with its pristine 200,000 acres of woods and waters.

After a series of turns and bumpy back roads featuring washboard ruts, we arrived at Nick's camp on Pemadumcook Lake just in time for dinner. I was nervous, knowing I would meet his parents for the first time. This was certainly a big step in our relationship, but

I was excited to move past the meeting and get out on the water to try my hand at fly fishing.

The family's single-story camp sat about thirty feet from the lake. Waves rolled gently onto a rocky beach. Inside, the camp was dark and a little musty, but still much newer than my family's camp on Cathance Lake. Nick's parents greeted us with hugs. His mom, a nurse, was short with short hair and a big, beaming smile. Nick's dad was tall, bald, and talked with a booming voice. I was relieved that his parents were so welcoming and easy going. For dinner, Nick's mom cooked fresh brook trout that Nick's dad caught that day, native twelve-inch speckled fish with slashes of white tipping their pectoral fins. Over rolls and potatoes, they reminisced about past trips when they caught dozens of brook trout. Nick and his dad discussed our plans to fish Slaughter Pond the next day. It all sounded dreamy, chasing Maine's iconic species on a remote pond with a fly rod and backdropped by the mountains of Baxter. They had hauled a canoe into the pond years prior behind a snowmobile and chained it to a tree. And I could use his dad's 5-weight fly rod.

The next morning, after a breakfast of coffee, bacon, and scrambled eggs, Nick and I practiced casting out on the lawn. He grabbed his dad's F.E. Thomas rod and patiently went over the parts of the cast: the lift, the backcast, the slight pause, the forward cast, and finally, sending the fly and landing it gently. I tried, but my casts were choppy and short, awkward, like a jockey's motion whipping a horse.

"Let's try on the water," Nick said. "It's different casting on water."

I was getting increasingly frustrated by my inability to cast more than ten feet. I wanted to participate in catching fish. Nick had me sit on the dock; since we'd be casting from a canoe later, I needed to get comfortable casting while seated. And he was right: Casting onto water and feeling the water's tension as I lifted the line felt completely different than casting on the lawn. I picked up the rhythm quickly.

Fly fishing for brook trout at Kidney Pond in Baxter State Park.

"Looking like a natural!" Nick's dad's friendly voice boomed when he came to check on us. "When you're in your back cast, hold the extra line in your left hand up near your face, like you're looking through a window," he suggested.

It was good advice. I was soon casting proficiently to twenty-five or thirty feet.

After a grilled cheese lunch, we packed for our adventure. Nick showed me how to break down his dad's rod—removing the fly, reeling up the extra line, breaking apart the four rod pieces and carefully wrapping them up and into a hard tube. We packed paddles, headlamps, life jackets, water, snacks, and fishing gear. We would return long after dark, so we prepared.

Giddy with anticipation, we piled into his truck and began the drive down a logging road. Dust kicked up behind us so thick I couldn't see past our tailgate. The twenty-foot-wide dirt roads were bordered tightly by thick forests of spruce and maple. Irving Paper owned the land and roads, but the company allowed the public to access them as part of a long-standing tradition between Mainers and logging companies. It was Saturday, so no logging trucks were on the road. If they were, you needed to drive very defensively, pulling off to the side and giving way to a fully loaded logging truck barreling down the road at fifty miles per hour.

Finally, Nick pulled off into an old clear cut. It looked like a tornado had ravaged the area—old slash was strewn haphazardly about while new alders were shooting up. It looked so ugly.

"Where's the trail?" I asked.

I scanned the area but I couldn't see any trailhead that might lead to a magical pond.

"We have to walk a bit, but this is the best place to park," Nick assured me. We got out of the truck and shouldered our packs.

Soon, we were walking down a well-beaten path through the woods, swatting at mosquitoes and black flies. It was May, great for brook trout fishing and black fly feeding. We hiked quickly along the two-mile path, anxious to reach the pond.

When we reached the pond's edge, I noticed moose tracks in the mud. I breathed in that boggy smell present at remote Maine ponds like this one. My neck was already covered with blackfly bites, but I didn't want to complain in front of Nick. He sat on a stump ten yards away and pulled his rod out of his rod tube. I wasn't sure exactly what to do, so I stood by and watched, hoping to pick up on specific details I could apply when I fished alone. Nick rigged our rods by first attaching the four ferrules, then the gold reel to the rod handle. He pulled the yellow floating line from the reel, the drag clicking as he pulled, folded it in half, and threading it through each circular guide. Then he pulled a fly box from his vest and opened it, revealing flies of various sizes, browns, yellows, golds, mayflies, midges, ants, all tied to resemble the real things.

Red and green canoes littered the shore of the pond, almost one hundred of them. Many were no longer seaworthy, moss trying to melt the aluminum and fiberglass canoes back into the earth. Clearly this was a popular spot, despite the long walk.

Nick typed in the correct combination and unlocked a green Old Town canoe from a chain around a pine tree. We flipped it upright and carried it a short distance to shore, loaded it with our gear and climbed in—me sitting in the bow and Nick taking the stern.

"This is perfect, there's no wind and no one else here," he said. "Let's head to the middle and start there."

The pond was seventy acres, a quantity I wasn't very familiar with, but was bigger than I envisioned. The more gradual west slope of Mount Katahdin loomed in the distance.

"Do you want a snack before the fishing heats up?" Nick asked as he unzipped his backpack and pulled out some trail mix and whoopie pies his mom had made.

"Sure," I replied as I carefully turned around in the bow and Nick tossed the snacks up to me. I ate the trail mix mostly in silence, taking in the peaceful pond, a light ripple on the water keeping most of the bugs at bay. Suddenly, a fish surfaced about fifteen yards away.

"Did you see that?" I asked Nick and nodded in the direction of the ever-growing water dimple, evidence of the fish.

"It's starting!" he replied. "There will be lots more. We'll fish until dark, or until we have our limits." I nodded. I was excited; maybe this wouldn't be that hard. I turned around and reached for Nick's dad's rod, then freed the fly from the small hook holder and tossed it into the water as I pulled some line off the reel.

"I put a red Hornberg on yours, just be careful on your back-cast—don't hook me!" he teased.

We cast our flies and Nick demonstrated how to retrieve them, in sporadic short pulls, causing the fly to skip across the water. After a few minutes, Nick caught a small brook trout.

"We need a net!" I squealed in delight, wanting to be a part of his success.

"Oh, we probably won't catch any fish big enough for a net," Nick laughed as he lifted the fish into the canoe and unhooked it. "This one is the perfect size for eating, the smaller the better, as long as they're over the six-inch legal length."

Nick removed a small measuring tape from his vest to confirm the fish was over six inches. It was eight inches, so he retracted his tape and left the fish on the bottom of the canoe.

We went back to casting, and more fish started rising. *It's my turn*, I thought.

I cast to one fish that kept rising in the same spot, but it refused to take my fly. Nick caught another, and another. *What was I doing wrong? Why wouldn't this fish eat my fly?* I switched it up and cast off the port side of the bow for a bit. Still no luck. Fish were rising all around my fly, some of them were even rolling on it, I swear, but none would bite it.

"Maybe I need a different fly?" I asked Nick, "what do you have on?"

"I have a Hendrickson on," he said. "Here, let's trade rods." He reeled in and went to his knees in the canoe, stretching toward me and passing the butt of his rod up toward the bow. I turned slightly and passed him mine.

On Nick's first cast with my rod and fly, he caught another brook trout. Now I was really feeling bad about my skill, but laughed it off, trying to make light of the situation. I enjoyed casting. It felt therapeutic, and I easily fell into the rhythm.

Nick had his five keepers at the bottom of the canoe, their skin drying out and their bright colors getting pale. He was releasing fish now. I took a break and ate my whoopie pie while Nick explained the difference between "wild" (naturally reproducing) and "native" (fish not the offspring of a stocked fish). Stocked fish could reproduce in a pond, and you would be catching wild fish. But native waters were considered waters that hadn't been stocked in twenty-five years or more, sometimes never, thus the fish had a more impressive bloodline. These fish were native, in case anyone asked me, as he further explained that that sort of distinction is important among fly fishermen.

After my short break, I cast again, and just as the fly dropped, it disappeared beneath the surface and my line went tight.

"I got one!" I squealed in delight. *Don't lose it now,* I told myself.

"Keep your rod tip up!" Nick coached. I held the rod with my right hand and stripped the line in with my left, as I had watched Nick do so many times. It didn't take long to bring the small fish to the boat.

"Turn around and I'll grab your line," Nick said and I did so.

He grabbed the leader and lifted my first fish on the fly up and into the canoe. Like most of the others, it was an eight-inch brookie.

"You're a real fly fisherman now!" Nick cheered. "Even these little ones feel big on a fly rod, that's the best part." He carefully climbed forward, handed me the fish, and snapped a photo of me with the beautiful trout. I was relieved to have succeeded and to contribute to our catch.

We continued fishing, but the action slowed. The peepers began their chorus after sunset. My fish count remained at one, but I was perfectly pleased.

"Well, we better get going," Nick suggested, and I agreed. "Let's break down our rods out here, since the bugs will be worse on shore."

Back on shore we unloaded the canoe and carried it back to the chain on a pine tree. Next to the water's edge, Nick and I gutted our fish with light from our headlights. We sliced from the stomach to the neck, ripped out the innards with our hands, and threw the guts into the pond. Nick packed the six trout into a Ziploc bag, and we loaded our gear onto our backs to begin the hike out.

The hike out took close to an hour, almost twice as long as it took us to hike in during daylight. Our great adventure was behind us and we hiked slower, careful to avoid each stone and root in the dark.

Sunday afternoon, we drove back to Southern Maine, a perfect Maine weekend finished. We were going to pan fry our trout for dinner with butter and rice. The fish I had caught. I was proud of myself, proud of my independence.

A few weeks later, Nick and I went our separate ways. The relationship just sort of fizzled out. And soon, I found myself back at L.L.Bean in Freeport, lamenting over the price of a fly rod for myself.

10

I AM NOT EATING ROADKILL!

"I am *not* eating roadkill," my brother Martin declared.

"It wasn't run over, just bounced off a windshield probably," I reasoned. "And it was still warm when I found it."

"You mean it's not even *your* roadkill? That's even worse. Get that thing away from me."

I delighted in his disgust, as siblings do.

Martin and I had always been competitive. Mom confessed to me recently that one of her parenting tricks to get both of us out the door was pitting us against each other. "Who's going to be the first one to the car?" she would challenge us. Maybe that's where my competitiveness started.

When I was in school, striving to be better than my older brother made me pretty good at a lot of things. Martin was the best male cross country runner, while I was the best female cross country runner. He was the high school valedictorian, and so was I. He studied engineering in college, and I did, too. Anything he did, I wanted to do—and really wanted to do it better. It didn't matter that he was a boy or that he was two years older than me—and no one reminded me. As a young teenager, I wore T-shirts that read, "Better than a boy," and "Boys are great, every girl should own one."

I also learned a lot from Martin. He was a perfectionist. He was studious and competitive. He graduated from the Massachusetts Institute of Technology and went to work for the government, including a stint at the Department of Defense. I saw what he did that earned praise and success; he was a straight-A student because he came home from school and completed his homework immediately. He practiced basketball and running constantly. I also saw what he did that drew criticism. He was late to school almost every day, and once he missed the bus to a cross country meet and had to drive himself to Belfast, two hours away, to compete. But aside from tardiness, he was disciplined, honest, and responsible, and he followed the rules. I also followed the rules. When your dad is a judge in a small town, you don't fear being grounded, but you fear his disappointment and publicly humiliating your family.

And now as adults in our thirties and back home in Machias for Thanksgiving, I was taunting Martin with a partridge I'd picked up on the side of Route 192. I inched it closer and closer to him, as if we were kids again. Although Martin was older, I was the wildly outdoorsy one. While driving home, I spied the bird-like body on the shoulder. It didn't look squished, but I was unsure whether to turn around and investigate. Curiosity got the best of me and I pulled a U-turn on the quiet country road.

Sure enough, it was a partridge. It was in good shape—well, besides being dead—and was still warm.

I picked it up by one leg and tossed it on the backseat of my Corolla, next to Argos, who was sleeping in his crate. When he smelled the prized game bird that we often hunt, he roused and began sniffing incessantly. I thought about what he must be thinking, *What the heck! Mom went hunting without me?* I was amused with myself the rest of the drive home.

Ruffed grouse is food for the Gods. It tastes like the most tender chicken. I prefer it more than bacon and ribeye, and the fact that it was roadkill wasn't going to stop me from eating it.

When Argos and I arrived home twenty minutes later, I tossed the bird on the lawn and had him retrieve it; might as well do some training right? After I was satisfied with Argos' fetch, I checked the bird's crop, a pocket in its neck where it holds undigested food. I do this with every turkey and partridge, because I find it interesting to see what a bird has been eating. This one had a crop full of beech buds.

I made quick work of cleaning the bird by stepping on each wing and pulling up on the feet. This left me holding the guts and insides, while the breast meat and wings remained on the ground. I inspected the breast meat for any bird shot, not expecting to find any, but wanted to confirm that it hadn't been shot. The breast meat was perfect.

I showed Martin the breast meat, which looked like meat you buy at the store. But he was not swayed. Mom grew up in Kentucky and her parents once met the *actual* Kentucky Fried Chicken Colonel himself. My uncle still lives in Kentucky and owns a franchise of KFC restaurants. I searched through Mom's spice cabinet over the stove looking for the famed mix of eleven herbs and spices she had brought back from her recent visit to the Bluegrass State.

I sliced the meat into pieces and waited for the cast-iron skillet to heat up. I soaked the pieces in an egg wash, then into flour mixed with the secret spices, plus parmesan cheese. When the oil began to dance, I added the nuggets to the pan. Although one partridge isn't much meat, my parents and I enjoyed it immensely. The golden-brown nuggets were juicy and melted in our mouths. It was the perfect appetizer to kick off our Thanksgiving holiday. Even Argos got a piece.

As for Martin? He stood resolutely by his belief that roadkill is not for eating.

Argos posing with a roadkill partridge we found.

11

UPTA CAMP

"See the birch trees? That's what you look for when pulling into camp," I pointed out to Travis as we neared the hidden driveway to my family's camp along Route 191. The radio station was giving the day's forecast in both Fahrenheit and Celsius. We were just south of Calais, which is probably supposed to be pronounced the French way, with a silent "s" ending, but we are simple and uncultured and pronounce every consonant. It's how we identify "people from away," which isn't necessarily an unfriendly term, just what we call people who aren't born in Maine, no matter how long they've lived here.

Usually Travis does the driving, but since this was his first time at camp with the invisible driveway, I insisted. The tight entrance, just past the crest of a hill, is unnoticeable except to the trained eye. Two dying birch trees are the only things that give away its location.

By this time, Travis and I were engaged. I had met him after matching with him on Tinder. Interestingly, a year before our match, I had matched with his older brother, Justin. I was looking for a boyfriend who hunted, so I suggested to Justin that we meet up for a goose hunt. My friends thought I was nuts.

"You're going to meet a stranger at four in the morning at a Walgreens parking lot and go hunting with him? He'll have a gun," they warned.

"Yes, but I will have one, too," I reasoned.

The hunt was uneventful, with some ducks decoying, but no geese (it was not duck season yet). There were no romantic sparks between Justin and me, but we became friends on social media. A year later, I saw Travis' profile on Tinder. The first photo I saw of him on his profile was one of him ice fishing, wearing a rabbit fur bomber hat, sky-blue eyes piercing the photo. I loved those blue eyes. Other photos showed him hiking and camping, and with a black lab. He looked tall enough for me (something that is *always* a risk with online dating). I also recognized Justin in one of his photos. I swiped Travis right and sent a message, *Hey, I know your brother.* The conversation progressed and Travis invited me to his house for dinner. I agreed. Our first date was a little awkward when, as Travis and I sat eating salmon, Justin walked into the house. Turns out he rented a room from Travis. Luckily, we all got over it quickly.

I put Travis' truck in four-wheel drive, pulled into the unplowed driveway, and his truck was swallowed up by the pine and cedar forest. Cars bottom out at this entrance, where the grade of the driveway opposes the grade of the road. A driveway culvert should have been installed by the Department of Transportation, like at the neighbor's drive, but even roadway engineers overlooked our secret entrance.

In the summer, when we returned with our boat, I would let Travis drive. A couple years ago, Travis and I bought an Alumnacraft fishing boat, eighteen feet long with a ninety-horsepower Yamaha outboard. One of the unfortunate parts about owning a boat is having to back up the boat trailer. He's so good at it. I joke that it's my favorite quality about him. But sometimes, when it's not busy, I ask if I could try backing up the boat.

Travis is a terrible teacher, he'd just say, "I don't know how to explain it, I just do it" or something similar. I heard that you put your hand at six o'clock, then move your hand the way you want the trailer to go. During one practice attempt at the Denmark Pond boat launch with no witnesses, Travis let me practice. There was limited parking so I needed to do a ninety-degree turn and fit it into a narrow pocket of space. I pulled forward and tried to back up the boat. On the first try, the boat headed toward a ditch. On the second try, it veered toward another truck. On the third try, it moved toward a tree. I was frustrated, but started laughing hysterically.

"Just let me do it," Travis said.

"Teach me to do it," I pleaded. "Tell me what I'm doing wrong."

He repeated his belief that he didn't know how to explain it. We both laughed and laughed. I kept trying, because I'm so stubborn, but never got it quite right. Eventually I gave in and let Travis back up the boat. He did it perfectly, of course, on the first try.

As we made our way to the cabin, I parked in a small clearing and walked down a steep hill, past an unlevel outhouse toward a small, green-shingled, two-story camp. The light from our headlamps sliced through the predawn haze. Beyond the camp sits Cathance Lake—at the moment, a vast and barren landscape, blanketed with ice and snow. I shined my light onto the small, recently reconstructed boathouse, and confirmed that no tree had fallen on it. Travis headed onto the frozen lake, pulling a jet sled that carries our bait bucket with three dozen smelts, pack baskets with tip-up traps, chairs, ice scoop, and Garmin fish finder. I headed to the porch, climbed the steps, and unlocked the door to the camp. The place had been empty since summer, so I wanted to air it out and check the mouse traps.

I unhooked the screen door. A rock the size of a softball holding the bottom of the door shut scraped across the floor as I pushed open the door. The screened porch is the gem of the camp, despite its thin, bouncing wooden floorboards. My family spent a lot of time there, just fifteen feet from the water's edge but protected from ravenous black flies. It's where my parents watched my brother and I swim when we were kids, and the whole family played Parcheesi. Today, we'd watch for flags from the porch.

I heard the gas-powered Jiffy auger sputter to life. We brought the auger because the ice was a solid eighteen inches deep, meaning it would take forever to chisel through by hand. The auger bored through ice to the lake water below in a matter of seconds. This particular auger is finicky and we hadn't brought it inside to warm last night.

The door to the interior of the camp unlocked with a little wiggling of a skeleton key.

I headed to the breaker box and flipped the master switch, then flipped on some overhead lights. An alligator skin hangs by the old wood stove, its history unknown. My great-grandfather, Oscar Larson, was a doctor in Machias and his patients often paid him in goods, so we suspect that's how the alligator came to hang at camp. But any kid (or gullible adult) who visits is told with conviction that the alligator came straight out of Cathance Lake.

Everything in the camp is original and was built by Oscar in 1922. A sign that reads, CAMP NOSRAL EST. 1922 hangs on the wall. Nosral is Larson spelled backwards. The door frame features his height in pen marks, along with his parents, and every generation since then, including mine. Except for electricity, no improvements have been made nor has the place been insulated. The original blue-and-white curtains still hang, albeit tattered and faded. There is a sink, but no running water; if you look down the drain you can see the ground outside. The cabinet drawers pull hard, and the windowpanes are warped. In the corner there's a tangle of rusty fishing rods with dried worms still on their hooks. I can smell the dead mice before I see them—one in each trap at various stages of decay. I'll deal with them once the ice fishing traps are set.

I walked up the narrow, too-steep stairs, to the single room above to look around. In the summer it is stifling hot up here, like most uninsulated attics. There are two iron-rung, full-size beds with old mattresses but no box springs. It smelled musty and stale. The beds were installed before the roof was built, my father explained to me once. I'd like to replace them with something more comfortable, but they would never fit down the stairs, so we would have to cut them apart, and that doesn't feel quite right.

If this camp were in Southern Maine, these two acres and the building footprint (which is grandfathered) would be worth hundreds of thousands of dollars, easily, even though the camp would likely be demolished and replaced with a more comfortable summer home. But the real estate boom hasn't reached this area. Washington County remains one of Maine's poorest counties.

I walked downstairs and went outside to set up my traps.

Cathance, deep and cold, was the first lake in Maine stocked with landlocked salmon, way back in 1868. Travis and I drive from Gray to ice fish Cathance annually, and we are never disappointed. Unlike lakes and ponds in Southern Maine, Cathance, given its remote location, gets very little angling pressure. It's not uncommon for us to catch a dozen salmon in a day, most more than two pounds, their bellies bursting with smelts, with no other anglers around to witness it.

I feel guilty visiting this camp only a couple times each year. Growing up, my mom, brother, and I spent weeks here with my aunt and cousins from Michigan, and my grandparents from Kentucky. Dad came on weekends, as work allowed. When we weren't swimming, my grandfather would sit in a lawn chair in his swim trunks and supervise the moving of rocks to stabilize the shore, or construction of a patio built with broken dock pieces that floated ashore in a storm.

Every August when we were teens, Martin and I would hitchhike from camp five miles to the blueberry barrens and spend the morning raking for the landowner. Dozens of us high schoolers arrived at the field just as it started to get light, grabbed a rake and a bucket, and filed into the next available rick, or lane, delineated by string. It was fun, hanging out with your friends. You were paid by how much you raked, not hourly, so you could rake fast and hard or slow and lazy. By late morning, covered in sweat with aching backs from bending over to pick up berries, and with our teeth stained blue, we'd hitchhike back to camp and go for a refreshing swim. Mom would toss a bar of Dove soap into the lake and we'd scrub the blue stains off our fingers and ankles. The stains never came out of our white socks, though.

By the time I reached Travis, the sun was rising, painting the sky gold and merlot. Suddenly, my phone pinged. It was a text from U.S. Cellular. My phone was connecting with Canadian cell towers. We were, after all, only a twenty-minute drive from the border. I ignored the message, knowing that if I end up with international roaming charges, they'll be removed after a quick call explaining that I wasn't in Canada, just close to it.

Travis finished setting his fifth trap, his legal limit set and ready. Each trap had a flag attached that springs up when a fish takes our bait and pulls the line. I assessed where to put my traps, considering my instinct and water depth. Our camp overlooks a small cove, and Travis' traps were perpendicular to shore, where he hoped to catch a salmon, and he had spaced them out about every fifty feet. I'd have to go to the left of his, in shallower water, or to the right, in deeper water.

"I'll go to the left of yours and that will leave some room for my parents' traps closer to camp," I announced, still open to Travis' suggestions. My parents would arrive in an hour or so, with Argos, to join us. Although they aren't avid fishermen, I got them lifetime fishing licenses a couple years ago, when they turned seventy, so they'll get to fish their own traps. Mom likes ice fishing just fine as long as she doesn't have to walk too far, and Dad loves coming to camp—he loves any opportunity to socialize.

"Ok, how about I drill your holes and you set your traps, so it'll go faster?" Travis asked.

I accepted his offer. I picked up the bait bucket, full of pin smelts, silver-purple flashes darting around in the cold water. We bought them from a 24-hour, self-service bait shop in Harrington for ten dollars per dozen, stuffing folded bills in a lock box on the wall. The owner trusts customers to pay for the bait he's worked so hard to catch. Smelt are great bait for salmonids, but are also notoriously fragile. I'm glad they've survived long enough to get a hook through their back and get dropped into the lake. We walked to the spot where I would place my first trap, and the auger started

My family with their salmon at the camp my great grandfather built on Cathance Lake.

easily, having warmed up. Travis drilled quickly. He pulled up the auger, and water sprayed over his boots. As he walked to drill the next one, I scooped ice bits out of the hole and cleared the slush so it wouldn't freeze up. Then I knelt to set my first trap.

I removed a twenty-four-inch wooden Jack Trap with a black flag out of my pack basket and stretched the leader, which had coiled a bit in the cold. I set the trap down and opened the bait container. The water was icy cold and the frantic smelts kept escaping my bare fingers. Finally, I nabbed one, hooked it in front of the dorsal fin, and plopped it into the hole. It was stunned for a second then started swimming in circles, trying to swim up to the surface. I waited and watched, slowly feeding more and more leader, trying to avoid a tangle that might tie it in knots. After a minute or two of frustration, I had about a foot of leader out below the ice, and the stubborn smelt finally gave up and swam down toward the darkness. I turned the spool on the trap, set the trigger, bent the flag down, and secured it around the O-ring. I gently set the trap down on the ice, bedding it atop the ice to anchor it.

I looked up to see where Travis drilled my next trap and saw him running toward one of his traps—the flag was up. I jogged over to help.

After a quick fight, pulling the line in hand over hand, Travis lifted a fat seventeen-inch salmon out of the hole. Its sides were pure silver with little black spots. It would taste good in the frying pan. Seeing the salmon reminded me, in part, why we keep coming back here. This lake, these fish, this cabin that I love, all of it connects me with my family, connects me with my past.

12
FIRST LIGHT FLIGHT

I don't consider myself a good duck hunter, but I don't let that stop me from chasing ducks. The only sound I can make through a duck call is a single "quack," and I hunt with a Brittany, not a retriever. Then again, I'm not your average hunter.

One early morning, my headlamp dangled around my neck, because the moon shone so brightly, I didn't need it as I walked across a marsh near Machias, toward the ocean. I love hunting in Washington County. It's about the size of Connecticut but with only thirty thousand residents and three stop lights. Downeast is sparsely developed, and the ducks are not pressured by hunters. Although it was a frigid fifteen degrees, I was starting to sweat. I slowed down. I was wearing bulky men's neoprene waders, carrying a layout blind on my back, a backpack on my chest, and my Beretta shotgun slung over my shoulder. In my arms I carried a small blind for Argos. I didn't want to sweat in those temperatures because once I stopped moving, the sweat would chill me.

I reached the spot I wanted to hunt in the small tidal cove and surveyed the water. A trickle of fast-moving water cut through the middle of the cove. I looked at my watch. One hour until legal hunting, ninety minutes until sunrise. It was an incoming tide and the marsh would soon hold enough water to attract ducks. Perfect. Outside the cove, the open ocean was calm. A slight breeze from the north annoyingly blew my hair across my face. I plopped everything I was carrying down in the grass and dug a few black duck decoys out of my backpack. I slopped through the mud in the cove and

Blowing a duck call. *Photo by Melissa Goodwin*

tossed them out. In an hour they would be floating. This area of Maine has one of the world's largest tides.

I quickly locked the pieces of my blind together and set up Argos' blind as well. I angled them toward the decoys. I gathered handfuls of marsh grass and tucked them into the sides of our blinds to help camouflage us. I continued brushing in our blinds until I heard quacks and looked up to see ducks flying overhead. I checked my watch again—fifteen minutes until legal. Unlike geese, which "sleep in," ducks start flying early, often before legal hunting time. Legal hunting time for the entire state is thirty minutes before sunrise in central Maine, but because I was much further east, the sun rises earlier, and thus the ducks fly earlier. I gave Argos the command, "Kennel" and he begrudgingly entered his blind. Although Argos loves pointing birds, he does not retrieve by instinct. But his instinct to freeze and be quiet around live birds is an excellent trait for waterfowl hunting, and he retrieves ducks with some coaxing.

I laid down in my layout blind and folded the doors down above me. I pulled on my facemask and laid with my 12-gauge down my lap, pointing toward the decoys. I wrestled with impatience and boredom and am tempted to reach for my phone to text and scroll and click. My normal workdays are full of hustle, bustle, and to-do lists. But while hunting, I must remain present, in the moment, ready for anything. The sky turned shades of watermelon and lavender. I realized with shame, that I would likely never watch the sunrise if I didn't hunt.

I love hunting alone. It forces me to make every decision—where to set up, when to call, when to shoot. There's no one to blame, and no one to shoot the duck I missed on my first shot, which means I always get a second and third shot.

A pair of black ducks landed in the decoys, and I dug through the layers on my wrist to check my watch. Seven minutes until legal. They flew off, with a few quacks, nervous about the unmoving decoys.

It was almost time, and I loaded my Beretta. My eyes scanned the horizon, with my finger on the safety should a duck fly into shotgun range. I appreciated this quiet moment, reconnecting with nature. For a brief time, I partook in what humans have done for millennia and become a player in this wild world.

Then suddenly I sat up, which pushed the doors of my blind open, and fired my gun at a low, quick-flying bufflehead. My second shot found the bird.

"Fetch!" I told Argos, and he leapt into the frigid sea toward the downed drake. Our morning was off to a good start.

Duck hunting in Downeast Maine.

13

AN *EXPERIENCE* HUNTER

"Tell them how much we love our dogs," Matt said in his slight Downeast accent, one hand on the steering wheel, truck kicking up dirt on the Wyman's blueberry land roads.

I was bear hunting with Matt and his hounds, and I told him I planned to write about the experience for *The Maine Sportsman*. I didn't know how I felt about the practice. Hunting bears with hounds sounds barbaric, unsporting, and dangerous. But I am an *experience* hunter (not to be confused with an experienc*ed*). I like the meat, and I like the antlers, but I like the experience of the hunt more than anything. I go places I wouldn't go, wake earlier than I want, see new things, and try things I would never try if I didn't hunt.

I met Matt in high school and for a while, he and his friend, Jason, balanced lobster fishing with running Wildest Dreams Outfitters in Cherryfield.

We pulled up to his first bait site and saw Jason and his father.

"Just a sow with cubs on the camera last night," Jason reported.

Although the practice is legal, no one hunts a sow with cubs. On the back of Jason's truck, six hounds stuck their heads out separate holes in a metal dog box. They yipped with anticipation. They knew what was going to happen.

Matt's father's voice came over the radio, "Nothing but raccoons here." It was a slow year for bear baiting due to all the natural food in the woods.

We drove toward another bait site when suddenly, like turning on a light switch, the hounds started howling. Matt slammed his brakes and quickly shifted into reverse.

"Do they smell a bear?" I asked Matt.

"Yeah, one musta been here," his voice trailed off as he jumped out of the still-running truck.

"Don't see any tracks. We could let the dogs out," Matt explained, bent low, still searching, "but we have no idea what type of bear we would be running. It could be a sow with cubs or a small bear."

Matt and I returned to the truck and drove on.

The group all met up at the last bait site. The camera showed a nice bear, probably around two hundred pounds, at about eleven at night. It was now eight in the morning so the track was pretty old, but we did not have much choice.

Matt let two dogs out of the box and put bulky GPS collars on them. The dogs that remained in the box loudly voiced their anguish—crying with jealousy and scared of missing out on the race. The two dogs, Mandy and Timber, were tall and athletic brindle Plott hounds. They got to work quickly doing what they love, running and sweeping through the thick forest near the bait site. It resembled a dance, the dogs trotting and turning, heads bent, noses to the ground, processing scent—discard or follow? They chose the scent of padded paws and black hair and tracked it like a magnet.

Within minutes, the two dogs were out of sight, yipping and howling. This meant they were on the track. Matt let out another four dogs, "younger and less experienced, but very fast with great noses," Matt said proudly.

Matt showed me his GPS screen, which indicated each dog's location. The collars not only monitor location, but a dog's barks per minute and what direction they are facing. We watched their symbols approach the Narraguagus River and stop, hesitant to swim across the cool water. Eventually they crossed and we received notification that Sherman, who had not barked all morning, was barking at forty barks per minute.

"I think they jumped the bear, see how tight they are?" Matt pointed out how close together their symbols were.

Matt started his truck and we drove toward the area where the dogs were heading. Then Norman's collar registered "treed." The collar can tell that he was looking up. His barks per minute were more than forty. Then Timber's collar registered "treed," then Sherman's, and the other three dogs.

The bear was treed.

We parked as close as we could, loaded our firearms and discussed the plan. "Christi, you stay with me and don't shoot until I tell you to," Jason said. "Even though the dogs started on the bear track we saw on the camera, they often cross a fresher track and end up treeing a different bear and we want to make sure it's a shooter."

"Sometimes bears don't like people and they'll come down out of the tree," Matt chimed in. "So I'll leash the dogs as soon as we get there."

"Dad, you get right under that tree and you poke that bear in the ass if he starts to come down," Jason ordered.

Then we started bushwhacking toward the icons on the GPS.

We hiked until we could hear a faint howling in the distance. My heart quickened as the howling grew louder.

"There!" Jason whispered excitedly. The black shape was not very high up the tree. She saw us and came down, running right past

Jason's father. The dogs were right on her heels and quickly treed her again, but this time she went much, much higher.

Anxious energy filled the air.

This was not the quiet, peaceful tree stand hunting I was used to. Six hounds were barking and howling, and an agitated animal looked down on us from forty feet up a tree. Jason gave me the go ahead. I squeezed the trigger. I missed. I shot again, and I missed again.

"She won't come down again, you can take your time. Steady your gun against that tree," Jason said as he gestured toward a pine. I did as he said, exhaled a deep breath and pulled the trigger of my .308. Blood sprayed the leaves, but the bear did not fall. She was slumped over and stuck in the crotch of the tree.

I was shocked. Now what?

Plott hounds ready to follow the scent of a black bear.

"I heard about this happening and wondered when it would happen to us," Jason chuckled. He and Matt discussed hiking back out to get a chainsaw.

"It's too far, it will take too long. I'll climb up there," Jason said. And he did.

Jason freed the bear and sent it tumbling to the ground. I walked over to the bear and touched her; she was still warm. I had never stood this close to a bear. Her black fur was thick and coarser than I had imagined. I looked into her mouth—her canine teeth were worn down from years of crushing acorns and beechnuts. I thought of Travis—he would love to be here in this moment with me. Later at home, I would do what humans have done for millennium: I would share my hunting story with him.

I was happy to have the bear fur and meat, I could share new meals with friends, but was not especially proud of myself. I hadn't done much except pull the trigger. I wasn't the hunter; the hounds were. The hunt was small dogs versus a large bear, and life was on the line for all of them. The hounds love it, live for it, and sometimes die for it. Today, most dogs are lap dogs. Is a German shepherd that goes on two twenty-minute walks per day a happier dog? Imagine refusing to play fetch with a lab. That is what it would be like for hounds to not hunt.

It speaks to the senses and skills of a black bear that killing one requires multiple dogs and hunters. Hunters use all sorts of tools while hunting—bait, scents, decoys, camo, calls, guns, and bows. Hounds use nothing but their legs and noses. They smell a half-day-old bear track and follow that track until they find the bear. Two equally matched competitors. There is no braver, more intelligent, or driven hunter than a hound dog. I have the utmost admiration for them and the handlers that make them part of their family.

The bear I shot while hunting with hounds Downeast.

14
TRAPPING TALES

When deer hunting season ends and the woods are soft and quiet with snow, when it's a struggle to get outside during the dark, cold, winter days—that is the perfect time to trap beavers.

I trapped my first beaver in 2018. When my good friend Jeff lost a few apple trees to the creatures, I volunteered to try trapping them. I care about his apple trees, too, because Jeff lets me hunt deer on his land. I shot a small buck there, my second ever deer, from his stand by his stream.

Jeff trapped beavers on his land years ago, but in recent years, he preferred to focus on ice fishing during the winter. I enlisted a mentor—a guy named Jonathan who I met on the Maine Trappers Facebook group—to teach me how to trap beavers. The three of us met at Jeff's house one Sunday afternoon. Jeff didn't know of any typical mound-shaped beaver dens in the area, so Jonathan surmised the beavers were likely living in a bank den—a den that undercut the bank itself. The three of us walked along the frozen tributary to the Presumpscot River in Falmouth until we found fresh signs of a beaver: freshly chewed sticks under the ice; multiple bubble lines under the ice, indicating a frequent route where beavers swim; and frost on the riverbank, caused by the breathing of the beavers under the bank.

When we determined what we were looking at was indeed a bank den, I chiseled a hole through the three-inch-thick ice and Jon demonstrated how to set a 330 Conibear trap. He strained to squeeze the large springs of the trap together. My confidence waned. If this rugged Mainer was straining to set a Conibear, there was no way I could do it alone.

"If you can't do it yourself, you can use setters to help set the trap," Jon assured me as he set the trigger. He then put a stick through it to demonstrate how it snaps down when a beaver swims through it. The trap was large and powerful. It made me nervous. Jon reset it and carefully lowered it down the square opening I had chiseled. I found long sticks in the nearby woods and Jon had me stick them in the mud around the trap, funneling the beaver into a route through the Conibear trap. That was it; now we'd wait.

Three days later, I woke up before my alarm. It felt like Christmas morning. I couldn't wait to check our trap. I grabbed my snowpants and chisel and drove to Jeff's house. Jon arrived early, so he and Jeff were drinking coffee in the driveway.

"Let's go!" I said as I pulled on my snowpants.

The stream had received a fresh coating of snow, and while our hole had iced over, it was easily identified by the sticks we had placed sticking up out of the ice. Jeff and Jon let me look first. I wiped the snow away and lowered my face to the ice, covering around my eyes to shade out the natural light so I could peer into the dark water. I didn't have to look long because a dark brown shadow blocked my view of the trap.

"I think we got one!" I cheered. Jeff and Jon looked down and agreed.

"Well, get to chippin'!" Jeff quipped.

I removed the rubber cover from the end of my sharp chisel and began chiseling.

"Don't damage the fur, chisel with plenty of room around him," Jon advised. Just as my arms started to burn, the beaver broke free. "Don't put him on the ice or it will stick," Jon advised as I pulled the trap out of the water. "Bring it over here," Jon motioned to the bank, "I'll show you how to release the trap and we'll reset it."

Jon squeezed the springs together and the trap released the beaver from its grip. "Roll the beaver in the snow and it will help dry the fur." I did what Jon said. It was a small beaver but its fur was thick and lush.

We reset the trap in hopes of catching another beaver, and headed back to Jeff's. "You can leave him in my garage and after work tonight I can show you how to skin it and then we can cook up some beaver backstrap for dinner," Jeff offered. "It's delicious, nice and fatty, unlike most wild game."

He was right.

In more recent years, I've devoted only one or two weeks a year to trapping. From scouting to setting, to skinning and fleshing, it's time consuming, especially during a time of year when daylight is short. The furs are not worth much, so I keep them for myself and do not need that many. One beaver pelt might fetch thirty dollars at a fur auction. The castor glands may fetch thirty dollars per pound, meaning around sixty or more dollars per beaver. Castor sacs are a pair of glands near the anus of both male and female beavers. Castor is usually used in perfume, but has been used to flavor ice cream, chewing gum, and many other foods over the past century. You won't see it listed on the ingredients list; it's included under "natural flavors."

Beaver fur clothing is biodegradable and the animals themselves are renewable resources. I have a hat and mittens, neck gaiter, shawl, fur ruffs, and a couple of hooped beaver furs hanging on my wall. I split and flesh the beaver tails and had them tanned into leather. I have a beaver tail leather wallet and have made earrings and bracelets myself.

———————

One year I tagged out deer hunting during the first week of November, so I started trapping early. Travis and I spent a weekend at his camp in Shirley Mills, outside Greenville. When Travis headed out deer hunting in the morning, I drove south to Blanchard to meet my friend Tom. Tom is a retired taxidermist from Poland, Maine whom I met when he mounted a partridge for me. The bird sat erect, wings out, neck feathers ruffled, as if he were courting a female. Tom is passionate about the outdoors and loves sharing his knowledge with anyone interested.

When I pulled off the abandoned railroad track-turned-ATV trail into Tom's driveway, he was outside loading up his truck.

"Good morning! Ready to check some traps?" Tom greeted me enthusiastically.

Tom, who is in his seventies, has been trapping since he was a boy. He built his off-the-grid spruce and fir log cabin in the 1980s. He felled the trees and peeled the bark himself. I climbed into the passenger side of his truck, and Tom explained that he had set about twenty traps for a range of animals, including coyote, bobcat, otter, and mink. After we checked his traps, we could set mine.

There was an inch of snow and a frost that morning. The woods were beautiful. Tom's first traps were just a few minutes down the road. They were otter sets along the bank of a small stream. We walked up stream to check the two 330 Conibear, body-gripping traps. Empty.

We continued along a forgotten road to the next spot, and I followed Tom into the woods.

Showing off my beaver fur neck gaitor and hooped beaver fur.

"Look! Fisher tracks!" Tom pointed to fresh tracks in the snow. The tracks were smaller than a dog but larger than a cat. "I bet we have one!"

Sure enough, about thirty yards ahead, we found a fisher in the #2 long-spring (foothold) trap. Tom dispatched the fisher with his .22 Ruger Bearcat. We admired the fisher; her fur was thick and dark. Tom reset the trap and headed back to the truck with his catch.

We were off to a good start.

We headed next to his friend's property. I unlocked the gate and Tom pulled his truck through. These traps were canine traps, meant for either coyote or fox. We could see the traps from the road, so we didn't need to get out when we saw no animals in the traps. When we reached the end of the gravel road, we walked down to a marsh and checked Tom's bobcat trap. It was empty. I noticed Tom had hung a CD hung from a nearby tree limb.

"Bobcats are curious and attracted to shiny objects, just like house cats," Tom explained.

The rest of Tom's traps were also empty so we returned to his cabin to process the fisher. Tom skinned the fisher, showing me how to split its tail and place the pelt on a stretching board to dry.

Then we headed back out to set my traps. We scouted a stretch of the Piscataquis River and chose a couple of spots near the town of Abbot. I set two 330 Conibear traps next to a beaver run. In the snow, Tom spotted a racoon track so I set a #1½ coil spring trap there with some anise scent as an attractant. Although my traps would only have one night to sit since I was returning to Southern Maine the next day, I felt good about them.

Sleep did not come easy. I was restless. Would I catch anything? A beaver? Otter? Mink?

On Sunday morning, Tom met again to check our traps. We checked his first, all untouched. My racoon trap was undisturbed, but I went two for two on beavers! Despite being November, their fur was prime. Back at Tom's cabin, we skinned, fleshed, and gutted the beavers so we could eat them.

The nostalgia of trapping appeals to me. Unlike almost everything else in this world, trapping has yet to be modernized—you don't use anything "fancy" or "techy." Just go out to the woods, with your wits and your steel, like the mountain men and women of the nineteenth century.

15

EATING BEAVER TAIL

I'd heard stories about eating beaver tail, but I had never tried it myself. I knew that beaver *meat* was delicious—fatty and tender and so tasty that I prefer it over venison. After I had trapped my first beaver back in 2018, I sauteed the backstraps in a cast-iron pan. The taste reminded me of beef, with a delicious, unique flavor. But the tail? I wasn't so sure.

Native Americans have eaten beavers for centuries. References to mountain men enjoying beaver tail are not uncommon, even receiving a mention in *The Journals of Lewis and Clark*. Beaver tails are nearly entirely made up of fat. Trappers who lived off the land during long, hard winters subsisted on lean wild game, so the fat from a beaver tail was likely a welcomed treat. Trappers in historical literature say that beaver tails, "fat all through, are especially regarded as delicacies." Another writer wrote that beaver tails were "highly esteemed by trappers."

So in April 2022, I decided to try it myself. My fellow trapping friends, Randy and Jeanie, came to my house because they had always

Cooking beaver tails over an open flame like the mountainmen did.

wanted to try beaver tail, too. They brought along tails from some beavers they had recently trapped.

I pulled out my copy of *The Meateater Fish and Game Cookbook* by Steven Rinella, found "beaver tail" in the index, and flipped to the page. The recipe was simple: Cook over an open fire. Season with salt as desired.

We started a fire in our outdoor fire pit and once it was hot enough, placed two tails over the fire in a grill basket. After a few minutes we heard the sizzling of the outer skin. Randy flipped over the tails. The leather skin was bubbled and blistered. After about twenty minutes total, both sides of the skin were cracked, so I announced that the tails were done!

After the tails cooled, Jeanie and I each took one and flaked away the charred skin to reveal a thick, creamy layer of fat. There was no meat, no muscle, just fat. We sprinkled on some sea salt and cut it into slices. Everyone took a tentative nibble.

"Not bad," Randy concluded.

"I kinda like it," Jeanie confessed, and I agreed.

It was very mild, but rich. Fat is delicious after all. One bone ran the centerline of the tail and holding it like corn on the cob, Jeanie and I chewed the remaining fat from the bone. It reminded me of eating baby back ribs.

It was interesting to picture us, a trio of modern-day trappers, eating fatty beaver tails cooked over a fire the same way trappers from centuries ago enjoyed it.

16
LOW TIDE

During the spring and summer, I go clamming. You can dig clams all year, but I'm too busy with hunting and fishing. Clamming is gathering—a kind of mingling, in this case, between hunting and fishing. Unlike hunting and fishing, I'm guaranteed to succeed, to always bring home dinner. I find it methodical, peaceful, and relaxing.

One day last summer, I gathered my gear to dig clams for Travis' birthday. I wore leggings and LaCrosse rubber hip boots. In the back of the 4Runner I put a plastic laundry basket, clam rake, and a hod (basket for the clams) that is exactly one peck, the limit I'm allowed to haul with my permit. One peck is almost two and a half gallons, plenty for a meal or two. I also grabbed those blue rubber gloves that lobstermen wear. Hanging on the basket are two measuring tools: one a PVC ring, two inches, that I use to measure clams (if it falls through it's too small), and the other is a stainless steel quahog measuring ring that you use to measure the hinge of a quahog (if it doesn't touch both ends, it's not big enough to keep).

I arrived just before low tide at Wolfe's Neck Woods State Park in Freeport around 11am. From the parking lot, I took the wooden steps on a trail down to the water's edge, the northern reaches of Casco Bay. I surveyed the flats. I saw turned-up mud where others had dug and left, herring gulls squawked and pecked at the clams the diggers inadvertently broke and left behind. It should take me only an hour to dig a peck, pretty slow compared to commercial diggers. From the land, I walked out onto the mud flats. My theory is that the farther I walk from the stairs, the better the digging will be, just assuming the area near the stairs has been picked over. I continued a ways down toward an osprey nest sitting atop a tall dead tree.

The walking surface was terrible—a soupy muck. I tried to walk up on the bank as much as I could because once you walk in the mud, you sometimes lose a boot, or kick up mud on yourself. It's a messy job. I smelled the tidal rot and a slightly fishy aroma of low tide. I saw the water line a few hundred feet beyond—and I remembered that once it turns, the tide would come in quickly. In the past when I started digging, I would look out to see the waterline far away, and then, getting lost in the job at hand, I would be surprised when suddenly the tide was lapping at my boots.

When I got to a spot that looks good, I walked out a little farther and looked for holes in the mud the size of a pencil eraser that indicate where, at high tide, the clam's siphon, or neck, was sticking out into the water. At low tide, they retract their siphon, leaving a telltale hole that betrays their location.

I found a few holes and started digging. I bent over and dug my rake tines all the way down, then I lifted the mud up and turned it over. I dug a couple of inches behind the telltale holes to avoid spearing the clam. I flipped the mud and looked, scoping for retracting siphons. Sometimes clams will squirt water and you can dig them out with your fingers.

I flipped over more mud and picked up my first clam—it was long and almost filled by palm. *A good clam for the birthday boy,* I thought. The shell was covered in mud, so I wiped it off. I inspected the shell to make sure it wasn't broken, that I found a living creature and not a whitened shell filled with sand. Live clams have blackish-blue shells. Since this was a good spot, I stopped looking for holes and instead dug the original hole bigger and bigger. I quickly had my limit.

Since I had been digging in the same place for a while, my boots were nearly cemented in the muck. I worked hard to lift my feet, to maneuver in the sticky mud that wanted to pull the boots from my feet. The mud made a slurping sound when I finally freed my boots. I carried my haul back to shore and gave my clams a rinse in a small tide pool. Back at my truck, I removed my muddy boots and changed into my flip flops for the drive home.

When I arrived home, I hosed my boots and gear off in the driveway and left them to dry. Since I rinsed the clams in the ocean, the mud was mostly gone from their shells. In the kitchen I put them in a pot with a wet paper towel over them and then in the fridge to stay cool.

For Travis' birthday dinner, I rinsed the clams in fresh water to wash away any remaining sand and grit before I steamed them. I boiled water for rinsing and melted butter for dipping while I steamed the clams until they opened. I placed the steamed clams in a large serving bowl and then Travis and I dug out the meat.

We slid the outer skin off the neck, and dipped the meat into the hot water, to give them a final rinse, then dropped them in the butter, and then devoured them, one by one.

Digging Clams. *Photo by Mathew Trogner*

17
DOWNEAST DOE

Washington County was once known for good deer hunting. In fact, the thirty-one-point Hill Gould buck, the state record, was shot in Washington County in 1910. But in recent years, most Mainers would agree that deer hunting outside of Southern Maine isn't as good as it used to be.

Even though I now live, work, and hunt in Southern Maine, I still have a lot of respect for Downeast deer hunters; they have to work hard. The deer are fewer and there isn't a food plot, cornfield, or article of SITKA clothing to be seen. Hunters still wear Carhartt and smoke cigarettes. Although every hunter I know loves venison, many Mainers living in one of the state's poorest counties have a significant financial incentive to succeed in the woods; they actually *need* the meat.

I had never bagged a deer Downeast, but always put that zone as my first choice for a doe tag. Finally in 2022, I got a doe permit. In recent years, due to intentional feeding, the number of does wandering the paved streets of Machias and bedding in backyards has exploded. I teased Mom that I might shoot a doe that beds in her backyard. At first, seeing so many deer was exciting, and she scoffed at my joke, but one year she actually said to me, "You know, I wouldn't mind if you took one or two. I can't have a garden anymore and they don't even move out of the road when you're driving!"

I knew deer had increased to "nuisance" status if Mom was warming up to my joke.

While I was home for Thanksgiving, my childhood friend Austin invited me to hunt some land he owned on the outskirts of town. We had both shot our bucks for the season.

Thanksgiving morning, in the biting wind, Austin and I sat in his two-person tree stand. We whispered about the deer he had shot from the stand the previous week and wiped our runny noses. By mid-morning, we surrendered to the wind and headed for the truck. On the ride back to my car, he pointed out the land he owned, showing me where I could hunt without him in the coming days.

The Saturday after Thanksgiving is always the last day of the firearm season. I sat by myself near Foss Point in Kennebec, named after my ancestors who settled in the area in 1765. I watched the field shimmer as the sun rose and the light danced off the frost. Eventually a doe wandered into sight about one hundred yards away. I peered through my binoculars to judge her size. A lone doe can be hard to judge. Her face didn't look "chubby" like the face of a yearling or this year's deer, so I decided she was a shooter. Then four more walked into the field. They all seemed about the same size. I adjusted my shooting stick up and dialed in my scope. When the first doe stood broadside, I took a deep breath and squeezed the trigger steadily on the exhale, just as Whitney's dad taught me twenty years earlier. The other does ran off to the right, but my doe ran to the left about forty yards and then fell over, stone dead.

I called Austin on my cell phone, "I got a doe!"

"You did?! Can you load 'er up yourself?" Austin asked. "We gotta go help Leroy, he just shot a buck."

"Yeah I think so, I have my jet sled. I'll meet you at your driveway."

I hustled and struggled to get the undressed doe into the jet sled, and then into my 4Runner by myself. I drove to Austin's camp and jumped in the truck with him. I recounted my hunt as we drove down the road to meet up with Leroy.

We bumped down a gravel road until we spotted Matt, nick-named Leroy, smoking a cigarette at the edge of a crimson blueberry barren. He jumped in with us.

"Where's your deer?" I asked.

"Oh, he's up on the hill," he replied. "I was givin' him a minute. He came out hot chasing a doe across the barrens, and since it's the last day of the season I wasn't going to be too picky; he's a six pointer."

I shared my doe story with him and we walked up to the dead buck. Austin patted Leroy on the back, "That's a great buck, bud." Two dead deer within minutes of each other. The boys posed for a photo and as I took it, we heard a single gunshot echo through the air.

"That's Brent!" exclaimed Austin, "I know that's Brent, that came from the direction of his shack."

We loaded Leroy's buck and drove the short distance to where Brent was hunting. Brent was outside of his shack, rifle over his shoulder, waiting for us.

"Eight pointer was standing there when I shot and he ran to the woods over there," Brent recounted. "The sun was low, kind of in my eyes though, so I don't know if I got him."

The four of us walked to where the buck had stood. We didn't see any blood, but followed Brent to the area where he saw the buck run. We spread out slightly, slowly searching for little specks of red.

"I got blood," Leroy pointed.

Austin, Brent, and I walked to Leroy, and then spread out a bit to look for the next drop. My stomach was in knots for Brent.

"Maybe we should call a tracking dog," I suggested.

"Brent don't miss," Austin assured me, bent over and studying the leaves. Maybe, but I was nervous. I knew what it felt like to wound a deer.

"Blood over here," Brent announced, and we gathered around him again, and searched again. I occasionally looked up, hoping to spot the deer, maybe standing wounded, or lying dead.

"These leaves are all tracked up, I bet he came through here," Austin suggested.

"Is that a deer?" Leroy asked. I looked in the direction he was looking, but I didn't see anything. He walked forward about thirty yards.

"Here he is!"

The buck had run nearly one hundred yards before dying.

"What a morning for deer hunting!" Austin put his arm around Brent, while Leroy lifted the head of the buck and I high-fived Brent.

"That's a great buck!" I said to Brent. "Can I gut it?"

I liked the practice.

"I've never had a girl gut my deer," Brent laughed, "but I support equality, so go for it!"

While gutting the deer, I realized Brent shot it in the heart and it still ran one hundred yards before dying! I was impressed by the strength of these animals.

Back at camp, it was time to gut my doe and Leroy's buck. I offered and gutted those deer too, because, after all, this was the community that raised me to believe girls could do everything boys could do.

With three deer and four hunters loaded into Austin's diesel, we headed to see his neighbor. We gave the neighbor a heart and a liver from one of the deer in exchange for use of his hose, which he had not yet winterized. We rinsed the cavities of each deer, my jet sled, and the bed of Austin's pickup truck. The neighbor's chickens were delighted in the bloody run off and assertively picked at the meat bits left in the driveway.

My friends Austin and Matt with Matt's buck.

We piled into Austin's truck again and headed across the dike toward the tagging station. But first we stopped at Tom's Mini Mart to gas up and share our stories with anyone who asked about the two bucks and doe visible with the tailgate down. The parking lots of Tom's and the Harrington Irving are places one can easily get caught up chatting for hours with friends and neighbors.

Deer hunting is usually a solo pursuit, but this late November day was full of shared excitement. The good ole days of Downeast deer hunting may not be in the past after all.

18

THE RUNNING OF THE SMELTS

It doesn't get more Maine than smelting. Cramped in a small shack, fishing for small fish—I love it. The coziness of the woodstove, the ease of just showing up and having everything you need ready for you. This tradition of fishing in the dark, retaliating against Maine's long, cold winters, is a welcome reprieve.

A couple years ago, my friends Jarad and Brittany from North Carolina visited Maine for the first time. Travis and I brainstormed things to do. We could go see some lighthouses, eat lunch in the Old Port, hit up a couple breweries, or go ice fishing.

"Let's take them smelting!" I suggested. "Even if the smelts aren't running, it's still a fun evening cooking over the woodstove and hanging out," I pleaded my case.

So we did.

And the smelts were running.

We arrived at Worthing's Smelt Camps in Randolph on the Kennebec River around five in the evening. It was an outgoing tide, and our shack rental was good for the entire tide, about six hours. Jarad, Brittany, and I stood in a muddy parking lot while Travis went inside the office, an old single-wide trailer, to check in and pay the eighty dollar fee. Worthing's rents about eighty camps and is one of several commercial smelting operators who rent shacks on rivers in central Maine. Unfortunately, because of the changing climate and, some say, removal of dams, the recent years have not been great for these operators.

"We are shack twenty-six," Travis announced, when he emerged with a plastic baggy of sand worms.

Our foursome walked down the nearly level ramp onto the ice where shacks lined the shore, each glowing with light. The ice cracked. The ramp would be very steep by the time we left, as the tide receded.

"Where we going?" boomed a bearded employee in his twenties, waiting at the bottom of the ramp. A saltier Paul Bunyan, he wore weathered Carhartt's and tall muck boots.

"Twenty-six," Travis replied and we followed the man through the row of shacks.

It was a Thursday night, and I could tell that the people in other shacks had been there a while. An empty bottle of Allen's Coffee Brandy sat outside one shack. Guns N' Roses blared from another shack, which smelled of barbecue. I heard cheers from a shack with a door open, and when we walked by, I spotted the flannel-wearing crew busy hauling up smelts.

"Here she is," said the burly man as he opened the door to shack twenty-six. The six-person shack fit the four of us nicely. The woodstove was already burning and our six-by-ten shack was warm. The shack was simple—wooden floor with six stools, while two long rectangular holes in the ice exposed brackish tidal water on each side. Hooks and lines hung above the holes, waiting to be baited. Two lightbulbs with exposed wiring hung in the center of the shack.

I grabbed a stool next to the woodstove as Travis cut one of the sand worms into tiny pieces. I baited each of my three Sabiki hooks and sent the line on my jig pole to the bottom of the river and reeled

Smelt shacks on the Kennebec River in Randolph.

it up a couple feet. Graffiti adorned the walls of the shack—names, phone numbers, and swears. Someone named Jimmy had caught twelve smelts the week prior, based on the tick marks next to his name.

I was setting the other lines in the shack when I saw the tip of my jig pole bounce gently. I squealed, "I got a bite!" and grabbed the small rod and started reeling quickly, bringing an average-size, six-inch smelt in the shack. Travis whooped and I hollered, letting the anglers in the neighboring shacks know we were on the board.

Rainbow smelts are anadromous fish, spending their lives in the ocean but spawning in freshwater. They swim up rivers in January and February to their spawning grounds, where they feed and wait until they spawn at the end of March or early April.

I love eating smelts; the smaller the better. The year prior I caught eighty-eight myself and froze most of them. When Travis

119

went out of town, I thawed out a package and enjoyed them all to myself. They're delicious and not fishy at all; in fact, they smell like cucumbers. I remove the heads and guts, then bread and fry them whole. The crunch from the bones and fins compliments the breading, and they taste like one big French fry.

I placed the smelt in my bucket and lowered the jig pole again.

"Put it on the bottom, that's where I caught mine," I advised the group. "And remember, Jarad and Brittany, it's tradition you have to bite the head off of your first smelt!"

A few seconds later, the tip of my jig pole bounced again.

"A double!" I laughed as two smelts emerged on my Sabiki rig. Brittany caught one next, but refused to bite the head off. Jarad made up for it, enthusiastically biting the heads off the first few smelts he caught.

Soon we were all on the board and began a good-natured hollering match with neighboring shack number twenty-seven. When someone in our shack caught a smelt, we hollered lies like, "It's taking line! Maybe it's a sturgeon!"

The inhabitants from the neighboring shack hollered lies back like, "That's number 942! We are switching to catch and release!"

We offered the shacks around us red hot dogs and cans of Moxie, and someone from shack twenty-five gave us a can of pickled fiddleheads and told us the secret to catching more smelts was to pour some Fireball liqueur down the hole.

The bite slowed down around ten at night and we left with eighty-five smelts, some empty beer cans, and another fish story.

19

I *NEVER* GET SEASICK

If there's a kind of fishing that is the polar opposite of smelting, it's tuna fishing.

"Where are we heading?" I asked Travis's dad, Mark, raising my voice, but not quite yelling, so he could hear me over the roar of the diesel engine.

"The Nubble," Mark replied, then made eye contact with Travis and grinned. I had a feeling they were joshing me, but I didn't really care where we were going. I was more concerned how long this loud, rough ride would last. Each time the thirty seven-foot Duffy lobster boat crashed down off a wave, I felt my spine compress. I figured I was already an inch shorter. The boat was named *Mufasa* after the lion in the Disney movie "Lion King" and features a painting of the character on the stern. It was an inside joke with Mark, and I never got to the bottom of the boat's naming.

"How far out is it?" I was yelling now.

"Oh, maybe twelve miles, at least an hour in these seas," Mark hollered back. "Should be there around sunset."

I decided I could lose a few inches anyway and the rough ride would be forgotten after we got rich selling bluefin tuna to Japan for sushi. A single bluefin can sell for a few thousand dollars to seventy thousand dollars. As a type of publicity stunt in Japan, the first bluefin of the season typically sells for much more. Some years the price can top three million dollars! A more common price is two to eight thousand dollars, although after considering the required boat maintenance, fuel, and docking fees, it is not really a get-rich-quick endeavor.

"You don't get sick, do ya?" Mark asked.

"Never have," I bragged, confident I had escaped the seasickness affliction. He was the third person to ask me that today and every time I answered, my confidence waned as I watched the sight of land shrink in the distance while we chugged offshore. The forecast called for three-to-five-foot seas, which is the roughest weather we would go out in. Anything worse would be unsafe. It was not my first time tuna fishing, but it was the roughest seas I had ever been out on.

Finally, Mark throttled down the engine. I looked around. The Nubble (or wherever we were) looked no different than the rest of the Atlantic Ocean. I couldn't see any land, rocks, or buoys, just an endless blue expanse that looked desolate, barren except the four other boats tossing about on anchors.

However, the depth finder told a different story—there was a ledge beneath us. The water was one hundred sixty-feet deep over the ledge, but the depth nearby the ocean floor dropped down to three-hundred-fifty feet. We were no longer moving, but my stomach started to feel uneasy.

"These seas seem more like six footers," Travis commented to no one in particular, just as a cupboard door banged open and shut with a swell.

I tried to distract my anxious stomach by catching bait while Travis and his brother Justin got the rods and leaders ready. I braced myself against the side of the boat as the seas tossed the boat up and down. It was dark outside and schools of mackerel circled the boat, attracted by the lights. I caught a few and then switched to a rod with a squid rig. The first seven-inch squid I caught squirted ink with displeasure as I hauled it over the rail and carefully placed it into the live well. Travis and Justin baited three rods with the mackerel and squid and then joined me in catching bait. They aimed the squids they caught at each other, trying to squirt each other like little kids with squirt guns. The deck was soon covered in black ink.

Through the darkness, I couldn't see the horizon. I inhaled diesel exhaust. My mouth started watering. *No no, we just got out here!* I begged myself, but there was no stopping it—I leaned over the rail and got sick.

"Good idea, chum up the waters and get the bait fish coming!" Justin teased.

After I puked, I immediately felt better, but the "better feeling" didn't last long. The queasiness in my stomach slowly built until I got sick again. I hadn't packed any seasickness medication because I had never been seasick before. I grew up lobster fishing, for Pete's sake. I once took a ferry ride from Spain to Morocco and laughed hysterically as items flung about the cabin and other passengers got sick over the rails. But sitting on anchor, surrounded by darkness and tossed about by large seas required a different type of strong stomach. I wasn't laughing this time.

"Do you have any Dramamine?" I asked Travis.

"No. None of us get seasick, sorry babe," Travis replied sheepishly.

I crawled down below to a bunk and curled up in the fetal position to rest. But I couldn't escape the relentless seas. I swallowed my pride and I threw up everything else.

All.

Night.

Long.

Morning finally came and, although the seas had settled, my stomach had not. Travis and Justin were napping, exhausted from tending lines and catching bait nearly the entire night. Mark was enjoying a Pop-Tart, watching the fish finder, and listening to ground fishermen chatter on the VHF radio about haddock fishing and whether the state was ever going to open up cod fishing again since there seemed to be plenty of them around.

Hoping that ground fishing would be a good distraction, I opened the live well in the deck of the boat and netted a dead mackerel the squid had nibbled on during the night. I cut a piece of the mackerel and put it on a hook attached to a short, stiff St. Croix jigging rod. I released the drag and a pinecone-size lead weight sent my bait to the ocean floor, one hundred seventy feet away. When I felt the line go slack, meaning the weight had reached the bottom, I cranked the reel up a few turns to take the slack out of the line. When I felt my line get heavy, I stuck the butt of my rod in my stomach and reeled in a fish. It seemed to take forever to bring a fish up from nearly two hundred feet and my arms burned even though it was only a four pound fish. I lost a few fish on their way up, kept a few haddock, and released a dogfish before getting sick again.

The fish finder beeped.

Mark shouted, "Tuna, eighty feet down!" I turned and studied the mark on the screen.

You can tell it's a tuna on screen because the mark on the finder looks like an upside-down U or check mark in the middle of the water column. Sharks on the other hand look like a straight line, and bait looks like a big ball.

When I looked back at the rods, one of them swung abruptly ninety degrees and bent straight over with the line screaming off the reel.

"We're on!" Mark and I yelled at the same time. Travis and Justin quickly emerged from their bunks, looking sleepy and alert at the same time.

Fighting a bluefin tuna.

Mark started the engine and threw the anchor line—marked with a buoy—overboard to free the boat. Justin ran to the rod and, before reeling, waited for the fish to stop taking line.

Travis and I hastily reeled up the other two rods, unhooked the squids and threw them back in the live well. We moved the rods to the side of the boat, out of the way.

"Let's go!" Justin cheered.

The fish immediately took us into the backing, hundreds of yards of line in no time. Mark backed the boat toward it. Waves splashed over the stern as Justin reeled, slowly gaining on the fish.

I watched for lobster traps, our anchor line, and anything else the fish could get tangled in while we followed the fish off the ledge and out to sea. Travis, Justin, and I took turns fighting the fish, switching when our biceps burned. Soon, the other boats anchored on the ledge got smaller and smaller.

After what turned out to be my last turn on the rod, I threw up again. "That's excitement vomit, not seasickness vomit," I joked, trying to save face. In all honesty it was probably a mixture of both, plus anxiety thinking about losing the fish.

"Leader!" Justin hollered, when he saw the eighteen-foot leader line that was connected to the 7/0 size circle hook.

"I see color!" I shouted.

I pointed toward the light blue shape near the water's surface. After fighting it for thirty minutes, it was our first look at the bluefin. I strained to size up the fish; was it big enough? The fish had to be at least seventy-three inches for us to keep, and the refraction of the water played tricks on me.

"Definitely a keeper," Travis said as he switched places with Justin and the fish took a run, screaming line off the reel and the tug-of-war struggle continued.

I readied the harpoon and handed it to Justin. A few minutes later, Travis had the fish near the boat, just a few feet below the surface.

"Stick him!" Travis hollered.

Justin threw the harpoon javelin-style toward the fish.

"Watch out for that line!" Mark said as the harpoon line uncoiled from its basket so fast that the entire bucket was dragged toward the stern. A buoy the size and color of a large pumpkin bounced out of the boat, attached to the other end of the harpoon rope.

"Good hit!" Travis said to Justin. I felt a wave of relief, but things could still go wrong. Travis continued working to reel in the fish, but it was going much easier. There wasn't much fight left in the tuna with a dart inside it and dragging around a buoy. When the fish came close again, Justin gaffed it and held it alongside the boat while I wrapped a thick rope around its tail.

I sighed—we got him.

We swam the fish behind the moving boat for a while to lower its core temperature and bled him. Then we opened the tuna door (a small door in the back of the boat near water level), timed our pulling with an incoming wave, and the three of us pulled the tuna head first onto the deck.

The fish was stiff and smooth, too big to flop even if it were alive. Its skin was gray and midnight blue, with a shimmering iridescence. It reminded me of oil floating on the surface of water when you first start your boat after a long winter.

The tuna was nearly nine feet long and as heavy as a pool table. The biggest I had ever seen.

I continued to puke every so often as we gutted the tuna and returned to the ledge get our anchor. Since the daily quota is one fish, we steamed for home. I was relieved to get off the boat and stand on the stationary dock. I didn't puke again, but I hobbled around bowlegged, swaying as if I was still on the boat. We unloaded and cleaned the boat while we waited for Seth, our tuna dealer, to arrive. When he arrived, he hauled the tuna off the boat with a winch, took a core sample of its meat, and weighed it at six hundred pounds. He packed it into his refrigerated truck of ice and left so he could overnight the bluefin to Japan.

Maybe we would get rich after all.

A bluefin tuna almost as long as me!

20
THE MAINE EVENT

When people think of a Maine moose hunt, they likely imagine the rolling hills and logging roads of Aroostook County and not the barrens of Washington County. However, when my name was finally drawn to receive a moose hunting permit lottery in the zone covering Downeast, after eight unsuccessful years, I was beyond excited. I knew I wouldn't see many moose, given the low moose density in that part of the state, but hunting the area where I grew up, and to include my non-hunting parents in such a special hunt was a gift.

To increase my chances for hunting success in such a difficult zone, I hired Dennis Perry, a guide my parents knew through their work at the Washington County Courthouse in Machias.

My parents, Travis, and I met in Deblois the Sunday before my hunt near the end of September. The landscape was a mix of forest, commercial blueberry barrens, and a commercial peat bog, all open to hunting. On the drive, I delighted in playing tour guide to Travis. I pointed out the road to Schoodic Lake, where I frequently used the lake's rope swing in high school. I mentioned that the blueberry barrens turn red in the fall and ignored him when he replied dryly, "I can see that."

Dennis met us at his off-grid camp, showed us the outhouse and generator, and went over the game plan. Dennis is tall and rugged and always excited. He talked a mile a minute with a thick Downeast accent. After a game of cribbage (Travis won, per usual, and teased me about losing, per usual), we turned off the generator and went to bed. Travis and I slept in the loft, while my parents slept downstairs. Dennis said he would pick us up at five in the morning, so I set the alarm for four-fifteen.

Travis and I had rehashed our game plan ad nauseam since my name was drawn in the lottery three months earlier. At the core of our plan was this: I would shoot first and then he could shoot right after me. On the first day, if we saw a young bull with spike antlers, we would pass him up, but by Tuesday, any moose was fair game. This was my first moose hunt and I didn't want to go home empty-handed. I could be more selective on my second moose hunt, I decided.

When my name was drawn in the lottery, I immediately felt the pressure of what could be a once-in-a-lifetime hunt. Many older Maine hunters lament that they or their uncle or their grandfather waited for decades before their names were drawn. They, of course, believed the system was rigged. I had just six days to kill a moose and fill my freezer. If I failed, I would likely need to wait at least another eight years before getting a second chance. And who knows what the moose population and moose management might look like by then, given the effects of climate change, ticks, and development. Overall, moose hunting in Maine has a nearly 70 percent success rate; it would be embarrassing to not get one.

On Monday morning we woke and fried deer sausage for breakfast. Dennis arrived at five sharp, fully awake, caffeinated, and talking quickly, clearly excited for the day. Travis and I jumped into his truck, but my parents said they were heading back to sleep. Although

I was happy to have them share the experience, they aren't hunters and they're in their seventies, so I decided they shouldn't actually go out on the hunt with us. They would go to work every day, but spend nights at the camp with us and make dinner. They would anxiously wait for that "We did it!" phone call from us.

We drove ten minutes to an old dead-end logging road, got out, sprayed our clothes with a scent-free spray and walked down the overgrown gravel road in the darkness. Legal hunting time started at 5:46. At that exact minute, Dennis cupped his hands around his mouth, pinched his nose, and let loose with a long, high-pitched whine—a cow moose call. I stared at the thick alders choking out the road while also straining my ears, hoping to hear the reply of a bull moose. We waited ten minutes. No response. So, Dennis started grunting and scraping a moose scapula against a sapling to imitate a bull moose territorially raking its antlers. Still no luck.

Since I didn't hunt while growing up in the area, I relished any opportunity to hunt back home. I was proud of my roots and the deer, bear, waterfowl, and partridge the area held, and the overall lack of hunters. NO HUNTING signs litter properties in suburban Southern Maine and, while hunting, I often hear the rumble of traffic or the whine of a leaf blower. But the woods Downeast are thick and wild and quiet. The only NO HUNTING signs found in this area are usually hung because the landowners themselves are hunting, not by anti-hunters. There are few streetlights, and if there's a traffic slowdown it's probably caused by a lobster boat being hauled on an oversized trailer.

After another unsuccessful call, we walked half a mile down the path and called again. Silence. We repeated this routine, calling, waiting, and then moving, until the path disappeared into the woods. We headed back to the truck and on to the next quiet, dead-end gravel road to repeat the same routine.

By midday, we were on our fourth abandoned gravel road when Dennis stopped and pointed to a moose track on the ground. "Two bulls were fighting here last night. This wasn't here when I scouted here yesterday."

I could see deep ruts in the gravel and chunks of moose hair from the fight.

"Let's call from up there for a bit," Dennis said, pointing to a knoll just off the road.

As soon as Dennis began cow calling again, I saw movement about two hundred yards in front of us. And then a dark shadow emerged from the woods—a black bear.

"Shoot, shoot, shoot!" Dennis pleaded and then he let out another cow call. The bear stopped, stood on his hind legs, and looked toward us. He quickly dropped back to all fours and disappeared into the woods.

"Why didn't you shoot?" Dennis asked. "You got a bear tag, right?"

"I didn't think he looked that big and if I shot a bear, we'd have to gut it and go tag it, so that would take a lot of time away from our moose hunt," I said. "I'll shoot the next one I see if it's big and I get a clean shot."

"Fair enough," Dennis said.

We were hunting in prime black bear habitat, plenty of undeveloped land and streams, and lots of blueberries to gorge on, but I was focused on a bull moose.

As the day dragged on, it grew windy and our moose calls didn't travel far. Dennis decided to climb up a one hundred foot high knoll offering an expansive view of a swamp and gravel pit below. Travis and I faced one direction, while Dennis stood about thirty feet away and faced the opposite direction. We stared and whispered. I tried willing a moose to emerge from the woods, oblivious to our uphill presence, but instead, near sunset, a large bear emerged from the woods.

"Bear, bear, I'm gonna shoot it," I said to Travis. He didn't have a bear tag, so he lifted his binoculars. I steadied my gun on my shooting stick.

"Cub! Cub! Don't shoot," Travis announced. I looked up and saw the cub emerge from the woods following the sow.

"Wow, that is so cool—they had no idea we were here," I said to Travis.

We watched the sow and cub melt into the shadows.

"We just need a moose to do that," I said.

We ended the first day with no moose. Back at camp, my mother had put a lasagna in the oven and waited for us to return. We recounted the day's events. Of course, seeing the three bears was the highlight.

It is going to be a good week, I thought.

On Tuesday morning, Dennis arrived at camp, even more excited than usual. He paced the room and just wouldn't stop talking. He had seen a bull in the road on his drive over, not far from camp.

"We are gonna drive to the end of the camp road and park there, then wait for legal light," he said. "Hopefully he hasn't gone too far by then."

Once on the hunt, we followed Dennis' lead. Travis and I set up with backs to each other. It was still thirty minutes until legal light when we heard a bull moose grunt off in the distance.

We heard a cow moan in response.

This is it, I thought to myself, *Dennis will call and the bull will walk out into the road and give me a shot.*

We listened and watched intently. Finally, the legal shooting time came, but the bull and cow moved farther away, despite Dennis' attempts to lure them in.

"The cow is probably taking the bull away from us, because she thinks we're another cow," Dennis said.

Time to move on. We packed into the truck and Dennis checked his voicemail.

"One of the guys at the peat bog called fifteen minutes ago and said there's a bull standing in the bog!"

Dennis threw the truck into drive and we raced out of the woods, leaving a plume of dust behind us. We sped across a blueberry field where irrigation pipes were being drained, water shooting into the sky in small arches. It was only a ten minute drive, but by the time we got there, another hunter was gutting a healthy, young bull that hung from an excavator.

The employee who tipped Dennis off described where the moose was when the young girl shot it.

"After the bull went down, I offered to get it with our machinery with the extra wide tracks; ain't safe to drive regular trucks or even walk on them bogs," he explained as he pointed to an old sunken piece of unidentifiable machinery, half sticking up out of the bog one hundred yards away.

"Well, at least they're on the move, must be startin' to rut," Dennis said. "Let us know if you see another one. We're going to move to our next spot."

After lunch of Italian sandwiches, we hiked down into a low point between two wetlands. Dennis spotted a recent sign of a moose: a moose had broken the ends of a sapling by raking its antlers.

"Let's try calling here for a bit," he whispered. We walked into the woods and found a good spot to sit. Dennis sat just behind me to my right while Travis sat against a tree to my left. It was a big lunch, I felt sleepy, and was just closing my eyes to rest when Dennis whispered, "Bull!"

I nearly fell out of my small tripod chair.

"Where?!"

I looked around slowly.

"No, I heard a bull grunting. Be ready!" Dennis clarified.

Dennis took his moose scapula and scraped it against a tree. He grunted, too. A few minutes later, I heard the bull grunt and could even hear the sound of his antlers raking against brush. Every few minutes I heard water slosh. He was getting closer. I took deep breaths and steadied my 7mm rifle against my knee. I stared at a thick group of alders standing about forty yards away that separated me from where I thought the bull was moving through the wetlands.

Dennis called again.

The moose grunted. I heard twigs snap. But the moose stayed hidden.

After what felt like forever, I saw the top of some alders move. I knew I would see the bull appear any second.

"Shoot, shoot, shoot!" Dennis whispered.

But I didn't see anything.

Dennis sat ten feet to my right. I leaned toward him, but still couldn't see anything. Neither could Travis. I leaned further and finally could see part of a moose.

"Do you see him? Shoot!" Dennis encouraged, so instinctively, after years of bird hunting, I haphazardly shouldered my rifle and squeezed the trigger.

I missed him.

The bull turned and retreated back out of sight through the alders. If he had taken just a few more steps, I would have had him.

Although it was exciting to call in a bull, it was disheartening to come so close and fail. In my head, I lamented the *what ifs* and *maybe I should have* scenarios the entire afternoon. The second day ended and still no moose.

That evening I updated our hunt plan.

"Travis, if you see a bull and I'm taking a pee, or I'm too slow to load my gun, just go ahead and shoot, I don't have to shoot first anymore."

I convinced myself that I had blown my only chance at a moose and kept beating myself up over it.

He must have seen me move or heard Dennis telling me to shoot.
I shouldn't have moved.
I should have waited.

Dennis shouldn't have whispered so loudly.
Too bad Travis couldn't see the moose either.

Defeated, I moped around the cabin. What made the entire situation worse was that it was a big moose!

Sleep came slowly that evening. And then Wednesday and Thursday passed without another moose sighting. I grew more grumpy and stressed every evening at camp. After a subdued dinner on Thursday night, we all went straight to bed. This is not how I planned on the hunt going. I wanted to tag out quickly and spend time with my parents, maybe go up to our camp on Cathance Lake, or go duck hunting or partridge hunting. I replayed the Tuesday bull scenario over and over again in my head. My stomach ached with anxiety. Travis stayed positive, but the long days were getting to me.

On Friday morning, we parked along a dirt logging road and followed a bear bait path to where we saw the big bull on Tuesday. Standing at the edge of the wetland, Dennis called, but the only response was a beaver slapping his tail. After an hour or so swatting mosquitoes, we returned to the truck to try another spot. Normally, as we drove along, my eyes were peeled, scanning the woods and fields for a moose. But today I was feeling sorry for myself and coming to terms with the idea that I would go home empty-handed. I took out my phone and texted a couple of my girlfriends.

Jeanie tried to console me: *At least you're making memories and spending time with your family.*

But I'm not, I wrote back. *They go to work every day and I'm stressed out every night. I'd spend more time with them if we shot a moose, then we could spend time together.*

I texted Emilie that time was running out and no moose yet. She replied that there were still two full days left, but I brushed it off. Physically I was still trying to kill a moose, but mentally I was pessimistic. By putting my likely defeat in writing, I began to accept and mourn my loss, the loss of getting my first moose. My loss of filling my freezer, and the loss of proudly sharing meals with my friends and family.

We continued driving along the gravel road and emerged from the dark forest onto the large expanse of blueberry fields. A low fog hung above the red barrens.

Dennis slammed on the brakes.

"Bull! Bull!"

I stopped texting and looked up. A young bull sauntered across the barrens nearly three football fields in front of us. Just when I had mentally resigned myself to going home without a moose, the bull appeared.

Dennis threw the truck in park and the three of us flung open our doors. With the truck still running and the doors wide open, Dennis grabbed our shooting sticks and handed them to us. Travis loaded his Browning 300 Remington quickly, but adrenaline kept me from loading my Ruger 7mm. I chambered one bullet but fumbled with the second.

Travis planted his shooting stick in the dirt road, raised the height, and began adjusting his scope.

I finally got my second and third bullets loaded.

"We don't have a lot of time, guys," Dennis warned, anxiously.

The bull lumbered toward the woods, unbothered by our presence. He was barely one hundred yards from the wood line now, about to disappear forever if we didn't hurry. Travis and I said nothing, we were hyper focused on our tasks.

"I'm gonna do a call to stop him," Dennis said.

I rested my rifle on my shooting stick and zoomed in my scope. The bull was still ambling, seemingly unalarmed. A few yards behind us, Dennis cupped his hands around his mouth and let out a loud cow call. The bull stopped in the middle of the expansive field, broadside, looking for the source of the call.

Without a word, but per our updated plan, Travis fired.

Through my scope I saw the bull flinch and begin to walk slowly. I took off the safety and squeezed the trigger. The percussion echoed in my ears. I couldn't tell if I had hit him, but the bull stopped walking.

"He's hit good," Dennis reported. He watched the bull through binoculars.

"Should we shoot again?" I asked.

I realized I'd been holding my breath. I didn't take my eye away from the scope, ready to fire again if instructed. I did not want to track a wounded moose or have a long pack out if we could avoid it.

"He's hit good," Dennis repeated.

Through my scope, I watched the bull take a few steps, teeter, and fall into the blood red blueberry field.

We high-fived and hugged. I finally admitted out loud that I didn't think we would get a moose. I took out my phone and replied to Emilie's earlier text: *We got one!*

She responded immediately: *Well that escalated quickly!*

I called my parents. They were on their way to work. I told them to turn around.

The three of us laughed and joked as we walked to our quarry. It was strange seeing the dead moose laying in the middle of a blueberry field. I had never seen a moose in a blueberry field and it certainly wasn't how I pictured moose hunting. His hide looked dark and healthy, his antlers long and spindly, not the paddles of older bulls. He was beautiful and grand. I felt sorrow, but not guilt.

We were snapping photos of each other when a blueberry truck came into view. When the driver saw us, he veered off the road and headed straight toward us, bouncing wildly across the uneven field. I was suddenly worried that we had done something wrong. The truck stopped and two Hispanic men hopped out showing us wide eyes and big smiles.

"*Alce*," one of them said.

I nodded and smiled back while doing the universal hand gesture for moose—putting my open, spread hands on my head to indicate

Moose hunting with my husband, Travis.

antlers. They nodded excitedly and took photos on their phones. Even though they spoke no English, and I knew very little Spanish, we shook hands and stood in awe and admiration of this giant woodland creature. With my rudimentary Spanish and Dennis' hand gestures, we asked them if they would drag the moose to the dirt road for us. With a warm slap on Dennis' back as if they were old friends, they agreed. A rope emerged and Dennis tied one end around the bull's rear feet and the other around the truck's trailer hitch. At the road, we detached the moose from the truck and thanked the workers profusely.

When my parents arrived, the gravity of the situation settled in. *When would I be here again, with my family, hunting moose?* I thought of my great-grandfather, whom I never met. He was the last hunter in my family, so I felt a connection to him. Had he hunted this area a century ago? I wished he could be here now, with us.

I thought about the meals I would share with family and friends for the next year. I thought about hanging the bull's antlers in a place of honor in my home. But first, I had a moose to gut.

21
YOUTH DAY

I met Abbi's mom, Heather, through Maine Women Hunters, the group I founded back in 2018. I wanted to connect with other hunters who had, like myself, found passion in all the various hunting seasons Maine has to offer. The group went on a hare hunt and we all instantly clicked. Heather stood out for a number of reasons, but mostly because she was funny and confident. Heather said whatever was on her mind and didn't tiptoe around other people or worry about hurting other people's feelings. In other words, she had a no-bullshit personality, which I appreciated and could relate to.

Heather grew up on a dairy farm in Windham. On weekends, she still returned to help her dad milk cows. I was curious to learn about their milking process so I visited the farm during the spring, excited as usual to learn something new to add to my repertoire. During that initial visit, Heather said, "Hey, Youth Day for turkey hunting is coming up. Abbi needs someone to sit with her. We've already got the spot picked out. Interested?"

I immediately accepted. Youth Day is a day reserved for hunters under sixteen. I had earned my guide license a few years earlier but hadn't done much guiding yet. Although this wasn't a paid gig, I figured it would be good practice to go through the routine. And it seemed like time to start returning some favors, given all the mentors who supported me as I learned the realities of hunting.

On Youth Day, at four in the morning, I picked up Abbi at the dairy farm. She hopped into my black 4Runner. It was a chilly morning, so I had the heat on, but didn't crank it too much because I didn't want to overheat. We drove mostly in silence to her grand-parents' house, but it was so early that even they weren't awake yet. We would be hunting their back field. Abbi was quiet as we walked to the field, and I could tell she was sleepy. She carried her 12-gauge shotgun and our folding chairs, and I carried the turkey decoys and blind.

We got to the corner of the field, and I set up the pop-up blind and decoys. The edges of the horizon started to smudge with the morning light and we heard a gobble in the distance. The decoys looked like faint silhouettes in the semi-darkness. I asked Abbi about school and she whispered to me about her new boyfriend. He doesn't like hunting as much as she does, she said. I chuckled and thought, *Well, that's gonna be a problem.*

It was legal hunting time and the sun was coming up through the trees, casting slanted light onto the green field. We heard another gobble, but it was hard to tell where it came from. I struck the box call, which sounded like a yelping hen, and a tom gobbled back, still quite far off. I waited ten minutes and called again and got the same response. The tom, still in the same place, seemed reluctant to come into our decoys.

By eight, my optimism was waning. We were hearing gobbles, but they weren't getting any closer. It's fun to hear gobbles, but there's no indication that a turkey will sneak into range.

I whispered to Abbi that we'd hunt until nine. After that it was supposed to get hot and the turkeys would probably retreat to the woods for shade. A tom gobbled again, but this time a bit closer. He was directly behind us in the woods, maybe a hundred yards away, no question closer than the calls we'd been hearing all morning. But again he called and it was clear he was hung up on something; maybe our decoys were spooking him or maybe he had seen our blind and became suspicious.

Abbi and I talked about what we might be doing wrong, that maybe our tom decoy was startling them or maybe they'd found a food source or a hot hen and didn't want to stray from either. The grass in the field was coming in well for early May.

Half an hour later, we were both scrolling our phones when a gobble startled us alert.

I looked up, and two toms were walking toward our decoys. They were walking left to right about thirty yards away and well within range, but Abbi didn't have a clear shot from her angle.

"Abbi, come sit on my lap," I whispered.

She shifted over with her shotgun already set up in her bipod and sat on my knees. I covered my ears with my noise protection earmuffs. At this point I feel like I had done everything I can do so why not try to get the moment on film. I opened my phone and hit record—I couldn't see the birds anymore with Abbi blocking my view.

It was a tense moment. I thought—what would I want someone to say to me in this situation? Not "Shoot, shoot, shoot!" because then I would rush my shot. So I whispered, "Take your time."

Abbi fired.

Her gun kicked.

"I got 'em both!" she said in disbelief.

When she got up and out of the way, I could tell she was right— both toms were lying dead among our decoys. And with that, Abbi's season was done—tagged out, two birds with one shot.

She was shaking with excitement.

She launched right into her recounting.

"They must have just walked in from the left together!" she said.

Still in the blind, Abbi called her mother, who was close by milking cows. It was fun to hear the excitement in her voice when her mom answered. I thought of my friend Jeff, who mentored me in my early years of hunting. He'd take me duck and deer hunting and he'd answer every question that came to mind. He seemed to know everything. Abbi had already had some success as a hunter, but I was still satisfied to help her get these two toms, her first double.

Taking my friend's daughter, Abbi, turkey hunting on youth day.

22
LOSING ARGOS

He had stopped dreaming.

That wasn't the first indicator that something was wrong; that was lack of appetite. But after Argos was diagnosed with lymphoma, his paws didn't twitch and he no longer whimpered soft barks while sleeping.

More than anything ever, I always wanted a dog. When I finally became a dog mom, I took it seriously. I got Argos while I was in between jobs so I could be home with him during his first year of life.

He was active and easy to train. He quickly learned the basics and advanced tricks like holding objects in his mouth, such as raw eggs (which he never broke) and bacon (which he never ate until I told him to). I encouraged him to point birds. Since I was a new hunter, we learned to hunt together.

Argos went everywhere with me, and I pursued hobbies that we could do together. He lay quietly on the floor, tied to a kettle-bell, at my Crossfit class. We went ice fishing and stand-up paddle boarding and even backpacked the 100 Mile Wilderness together. We tried many canine activities—agility, therapy, obedience, and trick competitions, and even a dog show. He humored me and won ribbons, but his only true passion was hunting. So he and I focused on the fields and streams and spent as much time as we could hunting partridge, woodcock, pheasants, and ducks. After every retrieve, he sprawled out on his belly with his back legs bent like a frog, as if to say, "We did it!"

When Argos turned eight, I began savoring our little moments together. Dogs die when they are eight and older so I didn't want to take him for granted. I smelled his fur and paws. I stroked his smooth, floppy ears. I took photos of us snuggling on the couch. We sat quietly outside in the sun. It's like I knew.

In April, Argos started seeing an internal medicine vet because of incontinence. Full bloodwork and an ultrasound showed no issues. At our next appointment in June, I told the vet Argos wasn't eating his dog food but ate human food. I thought maybe he had a cavity and it hurt him to chew his kibble.

I waited in my car while Argos was inside with the vet, per office policy. I watched a thin, elderly yellow lab walk stiffly across the parking lot. I tried not to judge the owner, likely in denial about his dog's poor quality of life. I'd seen my friends develop skewed perceptions about the condition of their pets, when the reality of their poor health was obvious to the rest of us. I vowed I would not let Argos suffer when the time came.

The vet called me inside. He compassionately told me the news—cancer.

There was no cure.

I was told to try and focus on quality of life over quantity of life.

"Chemotherapy would help the tumor on his liver," he continued, "but Argos would likely not live a year." He explained that chemo side effects in dogs are minimal, since the goal isn't to cure the cancer but to give more quality time.

Argos' tumor responded to chemotherapy immediately, and he was in full remission after just two treatments. However, after that second treatment he lost all energy and refused to eat. Travis and I decided to decline chemotherapy. It wasn't worth risking the side effects.

After a week and several trips to the vet, the chemo side effects wore off and Argos improved. I focused on all his favorite things. We went to an upland training facility and hunted chukars. He caught frogs in the lake at our house and carried them gently to the lawn where he nosed them and barked as they hopped back to the water. We went for off-leash walks and boat rides, and he played at doggy daycare.

His appetite never fully recovered, and he lost enough weight that he stopped triggering the seatbelt warning in the car. Every day was a worrisome game—what will Argos eat today? I checked the home monitor constantly while I worked. Without chemo, our toolbox was limited. I ordered tinctures from a holistic vet. I researched alternatives, like THC, and tried giving him powdered turkey tail mushrooms and colostrum.

During his final days, I took him clam digging and he pointed gulls and fought with green crabs. And his appetite increased again. He ate more food than he'd eaten in his entire life.

When I took him for a check-up, I reported Argos was active and happy, but had diarrhea. An ultrasound two weeks earlier showed he was still tumor free, so we hoped this was an unrelated intestinal issue. But the ultrasound that day revealed the tumor was back, along with lymph node enlargement. There was nothing more to do. I remembered my promise and made the final appointment for the following day.

Travis and I snuggled Argos in bed that sunny, Friday morning. We took him for an off-leash walk and he ran around, ears flapping, chasing chipping sparrows. He stood stoically at the bow of our boat while we did a lap around the lake. He pointed the chipmunk that lives in our wood pile. We went out for ice cream and he ate it enthusiastically.

Outside the vet's office, he stared intently at a squirrel.

Inside the vet's office, he died peacefully, a mouthful of treats, hearing me whisper his favorite word: bird.

I held him in my lap while Travis drove home. I stroked his ears. Travis dug a hole in the backyard. We lowered him gently and buried him with his favorite toy, a stuffed springer spaniel.

My friends were surprised to hear the news. "So soon?" They questioned. "He didn't seem that bad." But I couldn't wait until he started failing.

Food scraps go into the trash can now. The bathroom is actually a private place. The squirrels in the yard are safe.

There are far worse tragedies and heartbreak in life than having two months' notice to say goodbye to your eight-year-old dog. Yet, Argos was my life. I didn't have kids, so being a dog mom was a large part of my identity. I was used to our routines, used to him relying on me, used to his excitement every time I came home.

I lost him that day in August, but I lose him again every time I go hiking, hunting, foraging or fishing.

I dreamed of owning a dog my entire life, and now that is gone. But I kept my promise to him.

A few days after we buried Argos, I planted flowers on his grave. As I watered them, a frog hopped across the flowers toward the lake.

Argos was my best friend. He was so smart. He did everything I asked of him, even if he didn't really want to. I miss him the most when I walk in the woods. He was happiest bounding through the woods, exploring and always hunting–he didn't understand hunting "seasons." *Photo by Cait Bourgault*

23

ONE LESS FISH IN THE SEA

Unlike many little girls, I never dreamed about my wedding day. I wanted to get married but never pictured myself having a large traditional wedding with pomp and circumstance. As I grew older, I learned about the actual costs—the photographers and caterers and musicians—along with the stress and time it takes to plan a wedding. So when Travis and I decided to make it official, we figured an elopement would do just fine. My parents didn't mind, after all, I inherited my frugality from them.

When Travis proposed to me in 2021, I suggested we elope in Montana, just the two of us. Always ready for an outdoor adventure, he agreed, as long as we got to do a little fishing.

Montana has always held a special place in my heart. I first visited when I was thirteen on a family vacation. When my dad was in college, he worked as a bartender at Lake McDonald Lodge in Glacier National Park, so he was eager to share this beautiful place with his family. When I first learned that my dad had worked as a bartender, I thought, *Wow, maybe my dad is cool. Maybe he can make fancy drinks when I'm old enough.*

You see, having a dad who is a judge and a history buff is typically not viewed as *cool*. My excitement was short lived when he corrected me, that no, back in the seventies they didn't make fancy drinks like today. All he made were old fashioneds and Manhattans.

To prepare for that first trip to Montana, my family went to L.L.Bean and bought matching heavy hiking boots. We wore them around the house and around town trying to break them in. It didn't really work and we all got blisters, but that didn't stop us from falling in love with the towering Rocky Mountains that seemed to touch heaven, juxtaposed against endless sprawling plains. We returned a few more times as a family, and I spent one college summer working on the DeBoo Ranch, a five-thousand-acre Black Angus ranch on Blackfoot land in Valier. I assisted with horseback rides and helped brand cattle, but mostly I fixed fences.

Our elopement would be my sixth time in Big Sky Country and Travis's first. I planned everything, which seemed almost as exhausting as planning a regular wedding. The popularity of Montana and Glacier National Park had increased dramatically since the COVID pandemic with the growth due in part due to the television show *Yellowstone*. I made motel reservations and booked our flights and rental car six months in advance.

It was mostly a hiking trip (we ended up hiking sixty miles in five days), but we enjoyed some fishing. Glacier National Park no longer stocks its waters, but there are still wild and native fish to catch. It was July, but the glacier-fed streams and lakes were ice cold; we even saw some icebergs floating along. We decided to fish to our strengths—that is, our strength itself. We did long hikes and fished backcountry ponds where few other anglers ventured.

Our favorite hike was the Dawson-Pitamakan loop, a grueling nineteen-mile hike featuring nearly four thousand feet in elevation gain. Eight miles in, we took a side trail to Oldman Lake, a trail often closed for grizzly activity. We gave ourselves just one hour to fish since a long hike lay ahead. I casted a Black Ghost—a Maine fly, all the way out there in Montana—on a sinking line into the turquoise water and scanned for bears. On my second cast, I hooked then landed a beautiful fourteen-inch native westslope cutthroat trout. Travis caught a few as well, and we agreed this was the most beautiful place we had ever fished. We were in a bowl surrounded by sheer peaks that jutted up all around us. Mount Morgan hovered above us in a steep triangular point. The lake itself was teal, nothing like the color of water back home in Maine. The slopes around us were blooming with bear grass, yellow-white flowers jostling around in the breeze. Even though it was July, we could see patchwork snow a bit higher than us.

We continued our hike which brought us up to the Continental Divide. As we rounded a bend and I could see how far the two-foot wide foot path continued along a sheer cliff, I sat down and dealt with a mild anxiety attack. I thought about turning around, but Travis, as steady as a Grand Lake canoe, gave me a pep talk. He offered to go first.

"Don't look down or ahead, just watch my feet in front of you," he suggested. I did as he said and we did it. I even looked out a few times—the views were unbelievable.

We eloped on a smoky July 14 near Logan Pass in Glacier. I did my hair and makeup, scoped myself out in our motel room mirror, and Travis put a JUST MARRIED sticker on our rental Ford Explorer. At Oberlin Pass, we walked down a slope to a big rock overlooking the valley beneath and exchanged personal vows, in front of our photographer, Stella.

Travis, in his blue suit, went first. He told me he was so lucky to have me in his life. He hadn't written his vows down so they were short and sweet, which is typical Travis.

Then it was my turn.

I wouldn't say it was love at first sight but it didn't take long. Soon after we both swiped right, I realized every text and Snapchat I received I hoped were from you. You're a terrible teacher, very impatient, and way more high-maintenance than me. You blame me for things you can't find and blame me when you miss an exit, but you have a few redeeming qualities—you're really good at backing up a trailer, you clean my guns, you tie new leaders on my ice fishing traps. You are smart and hard-working and you are goofy.

Thank you for always loving me. You loved me after I puked all night while tuna fishing. You love me even though I bring home dead things I find in the woods . . . and on I went.

As I was reading my vows, Travis watched and smirked. Above us, tourists drove by hooting and hollering. After I finished, we went to different spots in the park for photos. From start to finish, the whole thing lasted three hours. It was low key and full of love.

Travis and I eloped in Glacier National Park, Montana. *Photo by Carrie Ann Photography*

The next morning, we drove to the DeBoo Ranch, where I had worked. The owners, Chuck and Cary, greeted us warmly and I checked out their new garage, and new bottle calves (calves that must be bottle fed). It felt like coming home. We jumped in Chuck's Ford F-250, and he gave Travis a tour of the ranch. When we saw a gopher, we jumped out and tried to shoot it with one of Chuck's .22-caliber rifles. It was great practice, shooting fifty yards at a small, moving target!

After a hearty dinner of fresh Black Angus ribeye, the four of us mounted horses for an evening ride as well as an unplanned dip—when we came across a slow-moving creek the horses swam us across. That evening we sat around the campfire and marveled at the stars in the dark, clear, endless sky. I thought about what had and had not changed since I was last here. Some of the horses were different, and my last name was different, but the expansive grassy plains remained unchanged.

24

I SHOT A BUCK
THE DAY I GOT PREGNANT

I shot a buck the day I got pregnant.

I had been tracking my ovulation for a couple weeks, peeing on a test strip, waiting for a dark line. Finally, on a Tuesday morning in November, my luteinizing hormone spiked—a bold line on the strip indicated that I would ovulate the following day. That afternoon, I left work early, as I had done the entire hunting season, to sit in my tree stand. I saw two does, but despite having one more doe tag, I was holding out for antlers. I shot a doe the week prior and Travis shot a small buck, so we weren't pressed for meat.

The next afternoon, I left work again at two and returned to my ladder stand. It was raining, so I attached an umbrella specifically made for tree stands above my head. I was cozy, despite the dreary afternoon weather, as I looked out over a field that hadn't been mowed in years. Twenty minutes before legal shooting time ended, a deer walked across the field. At first, I thought it was a spike buck, so I was going to pass on it. I pulled up my binoculars instead of my scope. Upon closer inspection, I determined it was not a spike buck but a buck with one antler broken off completely. He had also broken off all the tines from its remaining antler. The buck reminded me of the character Eliot from the kids' movie "Open Season." The regular firearm season was ending in a few days, and I was running out of days off, so I decided this Eliot was a fine buck for my first year as an Elliott and squeezed the trigger.

A few weeks later, when I didn't get my period on time, a pregnancy test confirmed my hopes—I was pregnant. We would have a summer baby due in August. We could host summer birthday parties at the lake where we lived. It would be perfect. Despite being pregnant, I felt the same. At ten weeks, it still didn't seem real, no symptoms, no physical changes. I had never yearned to be a mother, to have kids, which is why I waited until I was thirty-six. I already felt fulfilled. I was too busy, with too many hobbies and interests. And I was adding more. I just got my taxidermy license. I was supposed to work as a guide on two trips on the Allagash River next summer. But I do feel ready to slow down a bit. Travis wants kids and I am looking forward to it. It will be an adventure. Our lives are already changing—no paddling the whitewater Kenduskeag Stream Canoe Race this year, and no going on a moose hunt this fall.

When I was twenty-four weeks, I definitely had a belly—there was no hiding it. And I broke the two-hundred pound mark. My boobs definitely got bigger. I could feel little movements. I get heartburn sometimes, which never happened to me before. I peed a lot. I took naps on weekends, which is odd for me. I have always been a go, go, go person, but life will slow down with a baby; it's meant to.

I feel like a rotisserie chicken at night, just rolling side to side. I've had to slow down my speed on the treadmill at the gym. But I still lift weights and row at the gym. Rowing is interesting, given my belly. No strange cravings, but I eat more than usual. We decided not to find out the gender in advance; it is exciting to wait! Travis

Digging clams in Scarborough while very pregnant.

and I both think it's a boy, although I'm hoping for a girl. We have a boy name chosen—Oscar, after my great-grandfather—but can't agree on a girl name.

Last week, they told me the baby was one pound, nine-ounces, approximately, based on measurements. That weight puts the baby in the ninety-ninth percentile for growth at this stage. I'm tall for a woman at five-foot-eleven and Travis is six-foot-one, so the baby should, eventually, be pretty tall, too.

Of course, my hobbies are going to change when I become a mom. Travis and I can take turns so we can still have some solo time to hunt or go to the gym. But it seems like it's always the mother who gives everything up. And, as it should be obvious by now, I don't do things in a half-assed way, either, so I'm probably going to be a helicopter mom who reads lots of books about parenting and gets stuck mandating strict nap times. Travis will be a great dad; he's already a great balance of serious and silly.

We don't have any family leave at work. I can go out on short-term disability—even though giving birth is not a disability—for six weeks. I don't think a daycare will take a seven-week-old baby before they've had all their shots. And I wouldn't want to put a seven-week-old baby in daycare anyway. I might ask if I can take some unpaid time off, and then quit if they say no. It's frustrating that I feel like I have no choice, that I might have to give up my career just to be a half-decent mother.

———————

I can't wait to share stories with my baby, like the time I caught a twelve-pound Atlantic salmon on a fly rod in Iceland. Our little one will grow up outside with us. Initially, the baby will join us on the ice while we ice fish, and ride in a backpack while we check our game cameras. After a few years, though, he or she will sit in a blind next to us, and learn to pick fiddleheads, and learn to fish. Eventually our baby will play cribbage up to camp and hunt for turkeys from the ground blind. A forever hunting and fishing buddy.

Or maybe, in a twist of irony, our child will be a vegetarian who loves video games.

Our maternity photo. *Photo by Cait Bourgault*

ACKNOWLEDGMENTS

To my husband, Travis, who provides unwavering support, who reminds me not to overthink or stress about life's little things. Thank you for building me things that I find on Pinterest and humoring me when I sign us up to teach women how to ice fish or to do an Instagram takeover for a nonprofit. I can't wait for our next chapter—as parents.

To my mom, Carlene, who taught me confidence through example and that women can do everything men can do, usually better.

To my dad, Lyman, who taught me not to overlook the sweet meat on a clam and how to catch and release hornets from the windowsill. Thank you for teaching me to live honestly and with respect.

To my older brother, Martin, my childhood competitor, whom I was always a little bit behind, forcing me to constantly strive to improve. Thank you for showing me how to be disciplined and how to set lofty goals.

To my editor, Ryan Brod, who writes the most beautiful outdoor pieces I've ever read, whom I could never have done this without.

To everyone at Islandport Press — KJ, Katie, and especially Dean Lunt, who thought my story, this story, was worth sharing.

To Will Lund, editor at *The Maine Sportsman*, the first to believe in my writing.

To Dan MacLeod and John Holyoke, thank you for giving me a platform at *The Bangor Daily News*.

To all my outdoor mentors throughout the years: Jeff Miller, Randy Huntley, Tom Berube, Jonathan Hilton, Dave Conley, and so many others.

To the many badass female role models that have motivated and supported me: Judy Camuso, Linda Greenlaw, and fellow members of the Maine Women Hunters group.

To Argos—loving you was the greatest thing that I've ever done.

ABOUT THE AUTHOR

Christi Elliott, born and raised in Machias, Maine, is a Registered Maine Guide, Appalachian Trail thru-hiker, engineer, and outdoors writer. In 2018, she founded Maine Women Hunters—now one of America's largest female hunting groups—organizing group hunts, fishing trips, and educational and social events for every ability level. She graduated from the University of Maine at Orono. When she isn't working as a design engineer in Portland, she writes outdoors columns for *The Maine Sportsman* magazine and the *Bangor Daily News*. Her writing has also appeared in national publications such as *Ducks Unlimited, Shooting Sportsman Magazine, Kayak Angler,* and *Bear Hunting Magazine*. Christi works with several companies, including L.L.Bean, Swarovski Optiks, Old Town Canoes, Maine Cabin Masters, and AFTCO, to promote women in the outdoors. She lives in Southern Maine with her husband, Travis, and son, Oscar. *Always Game* is her first book. You can follow Christi's adventures on Instagram @christiholmes